D0205777

Parent–Child Interaction Therapy

Clinical Child Psychology Library

Series Editors: Michael C. Roberts and Annette M. La Greca

PARENT–CHILD INTERACTION THERAPY
Toni L. Hembree-Kigin and Cheryl Bodiford McNeil

SEXUALITY
A Developmental Approach to Problems
Betty N. Gordon and Carolyn S. Schroeder

Parent–Child Interaction Therapy

Toni L. Hembree-Kigin
Early Childhood Mental Health Services
Tempe, Arizona

Cheryl Bodiford McNeil
West Virginia University
Morgantown, West Virginia

Foreword by

Sheila Eyberg
University of Florida
Gainesville, Florida

Plenum Press • New York and London

Library of Congress Cataloging-in-Publication Data

On file

ISBN 0-306-44976-5 (Hardbound)
ISBN 0-306-45024-0 (Paperback)

© 1995 Plenum Press, New York
A Division of Plenum Publishing Corporation
233 Spring Street, New York, N. Y. 10013

10 9 8 7 6 5 4 3 2 1

For the developer of Parent–Child Interaction Therapy. . .
our mentor and friend,
Dr. Sheila M. Eyberg

. . . and to our loving families,
who share in all of our accomplishments,

Tim, Mom and Dad, Tim, and Jon (TLH-K)
and
Dan, Mom and Dad, Grandma Curry,
and Grandma Lingerfelt (CBM)

Foreword

The development and evaluation of Parent–Child Interaction Therapy (PCIT) has been a very rewarding aspect of my academic career, and I am excited to see the program detailed in this excellent clinical guide. PCIT is a short-term intervention with documented effectiveness that has much to offer mental health professionals who work with young behaviorally disordered children. After approximately 12 therapy hours, improvements can be seen in parenting stress levels, parent–child interactional patterns, parenting skills, child disruptiveness, and child compliance. Yet, prior to the publication of this practitioner guide book, relatively few child therapists have had exposure to this innovative treatment approach.

The development of PCIT began in the early 1970s. I had recently completed a doctoral program focusing on behavioral parent-training procedures and a postdoctoral experience emphasizing traditional play therapy approaches with children. Despite the wide theoretical gap between these two orientations, I recognized that each had valuable therapeutic elements that could contribute to an overall treatment package. It became an exciting challenge to integrate traditional and behavioral concerns. I was particularly interested in developing a child behavior modification program with strong relationship-based components.

The work of my colleague, Constance Hanf, had a direct influence on the development of PCIT. Hanf outlined a two-stage, operant model for modifying the noncompliant behavior of young children. The first stage emphasized following the child's lead and using differential attention during play sessions. The second stage included discipline components such as compliance training. A particularly appealing aspect of Hanf's treatment approach was coaching parents in the use of particular skills as they interacted with their children.

Hanf's basic approach served as a foundation for PCIT, but additional components have been incorporated over the years. For example, the play situations were expanded to teach parents not only the skills used by behavior therapists but also those used by play therapists. These powerful play therapy skills are employed to accomplish a primary aim of PCIT: to establish a warm, mutually rewarding relationship between parent and child. One of the many strengths of this book is that it provides clinicians with a thorough description of the practical, hands-on strategies used to enhance parent–child relationships.

Although PCIT has been available since the early 1970s, there has been only limited dissemination of the program to practitioners. I believe that dissemination of this work is particularly important now given the accumulating evidence of PCIT's clinical effectiveness and the need for short-term treatment models for very young children. The managed health care climate challenges clinicians to identify and use time-limited treatments with demonstrated efficacy. Thus, the release of this book is quite timely in that it may assist clinicians in meeting current and upcoming health care mandates.

In *Parent–Child Interaction Therapy*, Dr. Hembree-Kigin and Dr. McNeil have provided an excellent step-by-step guide for clinicians who wish to evaluate, treat, and document the effectiveness of their interventions for young children with behavior problems. They have provided sufficiently rich clinical detail to enable most child and family therapists who read this book to conduct PCIT competently. My hope is that the dissemination of this clinical guide will provide practitioners with an attractive alternative to less effective interventions, thus greatly increasing the availability of PCIT to stressed families with disruptive young children.

Sheila M. Eyberg, Ph.D.

University of Florida
Gainesville, Florida

Preface

There are already several good books available that describe the procedures for implementing parenting training programs and present the outcome research on which these programs are based. In our years of experience consulting with colleagues and students, we have observed that most are able to learn the "mechanics" of parent training from these resources. However, without direct mentoring by an accomplished parent-training therapist, few acquire the more subtle and sophisticated therapeutic skills that are the "art" of parent training. We were fortunate to have received this intensive mentoring early in our careers from a distinguished clinician, Sheila Eyberg. However, we recognize that such mentoring opportunities are limited for most mental health professionals. In preparing this clinical guidebook, it was our vision to go beyond the usual presentation of the mechanics of parent-training techniques and to explore the many subtle therapeutic aspects of parent–child interaction therapy (PCIT). In this way, we hope to disseminate key elements of the clinical mentoring we were fortunate to have received as we learned to become parent-training therapists.

Our overriding motivation in preparing this text was the broad dissemination of PCIT. PCIT is a short-term, empirically validated intervention that has wide applicability to both externalizing and internalizing problems exhibited in early childhood. We believe that the dissemination of PCIT is particularly timely given managed healthcare's growing emphasis on short-term interventions with documented effectiveness.

We are indebted to many individuals for their assistance in the development of this work. We are grateful to our series editors and friends, Michael C. Roberts and Annette LaGreca, who offered many helpful suggestions for the manuscript, and to our editor at Plenum, Mariclaire Cloutier, who provided us with the opportunity to disseminate this important work. We thank Jean Hembree, Katherine Newcomb, Steve Ondersma, and Ann DiGirolamo, who helped to clarify ambiguities and awkward phrasing and who encouraged us with their enthusiasm. A special thank you is extended to Kathy McGough, mother of Katie and Bridget, who graciously provided us with a parent's perspective. Much of what we have learned about working with families of young preschoolers has been taught to us by the hundreds of parents and children we have seen in PCIT. We are indebted to these families. The energy and resources for completing this book would have run dry long ago if not for the ever present love and encouragement of our husbands, Tim Kigin and Dan McNeil.

Finally, this book would never have been written without the tutelage and support of our mentor and colleague, Sheila Eyberg. We hope this book does justice to her work. Dr. Eyberg is to be credited for all that shines in PCIT, and we bear full responsibility for all shortcomings of this manuscript.

Toni L. Hembree-Kigin
Cheryl Bodiford McNeil

Contents

Foundations for Parent–Child Interaction Therapy

"I love my child, but I just don't like him very much." This common sentiment was expressed by the frustrated and guilt-ridden mother of a four-year-old child, who was seeking help in managing her son's disruptive and noncompliant behavior. She was typical of many parents who feel incompetent in their parenting role and acknowledge that anger, despair, and depression interfere with their ability to provide nurturance to their young children.

A two-and-a-half-year-old boy, "Sean," ran recklessly around the playroom overturning chairs and tables, stopping just long enough to poke a Lincoln Log in his mother's face and yell, "Stupid bitch! I'm gonna kill you! Pottyhead." She had come for help after awakening from a nap to find her young son hovering over her with a kitchen knife. Both were living in an atmosphere of multigenerational physical abuse in which the boy had witnessed his father's violence toward his mother. Sean was exhibiting serious aggression both at home and toward other children at his day care. His mother felt little self-worth and no sense of control over her life, and she interpreted her son's behavior problems as further evidence of her personal inadequacy.

"But it's not straight like yours. It's ugly. I'll never get it right," whined five-year-old "Kathy" while coloring with her father. Kathy was referred to us when her teacher expressed concerns about this child's anxiety, perfectionism, and self-esteem at a parent–teacher conference. The parents were well-educated professionals who held high standards of achievement for themselves and who had unknowingly passed on these values to their kindergarten daughter. They came to recognize the link between their own perfectionism and the anxiety and low frustration tolerance exhibited by Kathy. Although we see fewer young children like Kathy who are referred for internalizing rather than acting-out problems, aspects of the parent–child relationship figure just as prominently in the anxiety and mood problems of young children.

At the age of four, "Eric" was not yet potty trained and his expressive language was limited to two-word "sentences"; he communicated his basic wants and needs through gestures, whining, and crying. When he was unable to make himself understood or did not get his way, he quickly escalated to a loud temper tantrum. Eric had a history of serious medical problems in infancy and toddlerhood. His parents felt considerable guilt about their son's medical condition and did not want to "push him too hard" by setting limits on his misbehavior or requiring him to attempt self-care tasks such as dressing himself. They sought help when they recognized that their developmentally delayed son was not "catching up" as they had hoped, and that his behavior problems were worsening. The mother had to stay at home and care for Eric because four-year-olds in diapers were not welcome at day care, causing the family additional financial stress. Eric's parents worried that he would be unprepared to attend kindergarten when he turned five. These concerns are typical of parents who recognize that their young children are not developing normally for any of a variety of reasons including chronic medical problems, pervasive developmental disorders, and mental retardation.

The treatment approach described in this volume, Parent–Child Interaction Therapy (PCIT), was designed specifically for families such as these with young children who are experiencing a broad range of behavioral, emotional, and developmental problems. We view PCIT as a basic framework for treating many of the problems that arise in childhood between the ages of two and seven years.

THEORETICAL UNDERPINNINGS

When Dr. Sheila Eyberg developed PCIT, she drew from her broad background in operant theory, traditional child psychotherapy, and early child development (Eyberg, 1988). Dr. Eyberg was heavily influenced by the work of her colleague, Dr. Constance Hanf, who had developed a two-stage operant model for modifying the oppositional behavior of young children (Hanf, 1969). In the first stage of treatment, mothers were taught the technique of differential reinforcement. In other words, they were taught to give their attention to all of their child's positive behaviors and to ignore all negative behaviors. In the second stage, parents were taught to give clear directions, consistently reward compliance with praise, and use time-out for noncompliance. Perhaps the most appealing aspect of Hanf's approach was that she worked with the parent and child together, doing on-the-spot coaching of parenting skills. Eyberg is one of several researchers who have developed and evaluated aspects of Hanf's original model (e.g., Forehand & McMahon, 1981; Barkley, 1987; Webster-Stratton, 1982).

Although Hanf's approach produced clear and rapid behavioral change, Eyberg recognized that traditional play therapy also had much to offer these families, with its emphasis on developing a warm and safe therapeutic relationship. She found that just as parents could be taught the operant skill of differential attention, they also could be taught the traditional play therapy skills of following the child's lead, providing undivided attention, describing play activities, reflecting and expanding on child verbalizations, and imitation.

Eyberg's integration of operant methods and traditional play therapy techniques took place within a solid developmental framework. That is, PCIT is conducted in the context of dyadic play situations largely because "play is the primary medium through which children develop problem-solving skills and work through developmental problems" (Eyberg, 1988, p. 35). A developmental perspective is essential to providing effective treatment. Many of the problems that arise in parent–child dyads are related to developmental struggles for autonomy or inappropriate developmental expectations held by parents.

WORKING WITH THE PARENT AND CHILD TOGETHER

We believe it is critical that any therapeutic work done with a child of preschool or early elementary school age directly involve the child's caregivers. Parents have enormous influence over their young children's behavioral and emotional development, and some parenting practices may cause or exacerbate young children's problems. According to Eyberg (1988, p. 35),

> ...many of the behavioral problems young children present are established through their earliest interactions with their parents. Even in those cases where the child's problems seem to originate because of biological characteristics, such as difficult temperament, or neurological defects suspected in autistic, hyperactive, or developmentally impaired youngsters, many of the problem behaviors seem to be intensified by the interaction patterns between parent and child.

Just as parents may negatively influence their children's behavior and the parent–child relationship, they have enormous power to influence their children in a positive way. In early childhood, parents are the center of the child's world, providing nurturance, sustenance, safety, and learning opportunities. Preschool-age children are not cognitively sophisticated enough to reason independently, and the influence of peers is minimal. At no other time in childhood or adolescence are parents in a position to influence their children in such a dramatic and pervasive way as they are during the preschool years. In later childhood and adolescence, the influence of parents is overshadowed by the substantial influence of peers, teachers, romantic partners, and developmental needs for autonomy. The therapist's power to influence a young child in a one-to-one therapeutic relationship pales in comparison to the power of parents to produce change through their interactions with their children.

Sometimes the parents we work with express disappointment that they cannot simply drop off their children for an hour of "magical" therapy with us each week and expect their problems to be resolved. We explain that what we can do in one hour of individual child therapy once a week is a mere drop in the bucket in comparison to what we can accomplish if the parent becomes a "therapist" for their child at home, every day of the week. We also help some parents to recognize the economic reality that individual therapy is a long, expensive proposition, whereas most problems of early childhood can be effectively treated in a relatively short time using a parent training approach such as PCIT.

DIRECT COACHING OF PARENT–CHILD INTERACTIONS

We believe that the feature of PCIT that makes it so effective is the use of direct coaching of parent–child interactions. In indirect approaches, skills are taught individually to parents, are practiced at home, and then the parents report back any problems they had at the following therapy session. Direct coaching of dyads presents several advantages over the indirect method. First, parental errors can be corrected promptly, before they become well-ingrained through a week of home practice. Second, every child presents his or her own unique challenges, and the creative clinician can use the direct coaching method to make quick modifications as problems arise, modeling good problem-solving skills for parents. Third, many parents lack the confidence to use the new skills without the initial encouragement and support offered by the therapist-coach. Fourth, direct coaching results in much faster learning, as the therapist is able to shape the parenting skills by rewarding the parent for successive approximations. And fifth, parents are not always accurate reporters of their own or their young children's behavior. Relying on parent report of the skills they use and the child's response can result in inaccurate perceptions of treatment progress.

Direct coaching is both the heart and the art of PCIT. Nearly any beginning therapist can quickly learn the mechanics of conducting PCIT and will be able to teach the core skills to parents as they are outlined in Chapters 3 and 5. However, the challenging and creative aspect of this therapy is recognizing the subtle qualities of parent–child interactions that characterize dysfunctional or more adaptive parent–child relationships, and then translating those observations into clinically sensitive and effective coaching strategies. We find that the more we do PCIT, the more we learn about families and the more we add to our coaching repertoires. In Chapters 4 and 7, we present a vision for how a skilled clinician might go beyond coaching the standard set of PCIT skills to coaching parents in a range of complex interactions (e.g., recognizing and working at their child's level of development, making use of body language and voice qualities, encouraging child autonomy within developmental norms, supporting self-acceptance and problem-solving efforts).

NORMATIVE BEHAVIOR PROBLEMS IN YOUNG CHILDREN

Many young children engage in noncompliant, aggressive, and highly active behavior during the course of normal development. In most children, behavior problems peak at about age three and decline during the remaining preschool years. The nature of behavior problems displayed by normal preschoolers is clearly related to the particular developmental hurdles facing the child (Forehand & Wierson, 1993). For example, at the age of two to three, young children begin seeking independence and autonomy. As they work on these developmental tasks, they are likely to be noncompliant with parents and to have temper tantrums when they do not get their way. For example, doing things oneself, without parental assistance, is very important to a three-year-old. This developmental need can precipitate confrontations between the parent and child. Parents who resist allowing their child to pour his or her own juice or who cannot allow their child to wear a favorite summer outfit during the cold of winter may experience the strength of such autonomy needs firsthand.

Rates of child compliance in normally developing children vary as a function of how they are measured, but most preschoolers obey between 50 and 75% of their parents' requests (Schroeder & Gordon, 1991). As preschoolers develop greater verbal competence, the nature of their noncompliance changes from simple direct defiance to more complex negotiation to avoid or defer compliance (Kinzynski, Kochanska, Radke-Yarrow, & Girnius-Brown, 1987). Excuses for not obeying a parent's request often mirror the excuses children have heard from parents, such as: "I can't, I have a headache"; "I don't have enough time"; "I'm too busy right now"; "In a minute . . ."; or "I'll do it after I'm done playing."

At the ages of four to five, young children are expected to begin learning to play cooperatively with other children and normative behavior problems include aggression, difficulty sharing, and difficulty taking turns. Aggression toward other children declines as preschoolers learn more sophisticated means of solving problems through verbal negotiation and begin to learn to regulate their own emotions. These critical preschool experiences in learning how to interact effectively with peers set the stage for social adjustment in kindergarten and early elementary school.

INTERVENING EARLY

A common belief is that most problems that occur during the preschool years will be outgrown as the child passes through a difficult developmental phase. This is generally true for children whose behavior and developmental problems fall within normal limits of individual variability. However, there is mounting evidence that serious problems persist, placing these children at risk for adjustment problems in elementary school and beyond (e.g., Campbell & Ewing, 1990; McGee, Partridge, Williams, & Silva, 1991). Although a wide variety of oppositional and aggressive behaviors occur during the course of normal development, very few preschoolers display these behaviors at extreme levels. When behavior problems occur across caregivers and with extreme frequency or intensity, they are unlikely to be transient and, when they occur, are indicative of serious and persistent conduct problems (Loeber, 1990). There are some serious conduct problems that are rarely exhibited by preschoolers (e.g., persistent stealing outside the home, using a weapon such as a knife), and these are clearly indicative of a conduct problem that requires intervention (Campbell, 1990). Other indicators of problems that are likely to persist across the preschool years and into elementary school include significant conflict in the parent–child relationship, ongoing family stress and disruption, and multiple problems of great intensity.

For children with serious conduct problems, intervention during the preschool years is critical. Untreated problems displayed by preschoolers tend to get worse over time, interfering with their development of self-help skills, socialization, and early academic skills. Also, therapy during the preschool years may be more effective than treatments initiated after age seven. There are several possible explanations for this. First, problem behaviors in preschoolers tend to be less well-ingrained than in older children who have longer learning histories. Second, intervening through the parents is much more potent with young children as they do not have many of the competing external influences (e.g., peers, school) experienced by older children. Third, young children have fewer cognitive resources for questioning and challenging behavioral interventions. Compared to older children, preschoolers are more accepting of new behavioral expectations, and less skeptical when parents suddenly begin providing large amounts of positive attention. Finally, very young children with significant conduct problems still exhibit affection toward their parents as well as cooperative behaviors which can be shaped to occur more frequently. After several years of behavior problems without effective intervention, older children display fewer of these positive qualities on which to build.

DECIDING WHICH FAMILIES MAY BENEFIT FROM PCIT

As we mentioned earlier, PCIT is an early intervention approach that may be applied to a broad range of presenting problems in young children. Generally speaking, PCIT is appropriate for young children demonstrating: (1) externaliz-

Table 1-1. Some Presenting Problems That May Be Addressed Using PCIT

Noncompliance	Stealing	Low self-esteem
Verbal aggression	Hyperactivity	Sad mood
Cruelty to animals	Destructive behavior	Perfectionism
Physical aggression	Bonding in blended families	Developmental delays
Fire-setting	Self-injurious behavior	Generalized anxiety
Lying	Whining	Postdivorce adjustment
Classroom conduct problems	Abuse sequelae	Separation anxiety

ing problems such as noncompliance, defiance, verbal and physical aggression; (2) pre-conduct-disordered behaviors such as cruelty to animals, stealing, lying, and fire-setting; (3) inattention and overactivity; (4) internalizing problems such as sad affect, anxiety, low self-esteem, and perfectionism; (5) developmental problems stemming from mild to moderate mental retardation; (6) parent–child relationship problems in the context of divorce and adoption; and (7) sequelae of abuse and neglect (see Table 1-1). However, not all families are equally likely to benefit from PCIT and some presenting problems require modifications in the treatment program. In deciding whether a particular family is likely to benefit from PCIT, characteristics of the parents or other caregivers should be considered such as motivation for participation, intellectual functioning, and psychopathology, as well as child factors such as developmental level and nature of presenting problems (see Table 1-2).

PCIT cannot be effective without willing participation by parents, and we do not recommend this approach for parents who are highly resistant to treatment. We have found that some parents who are court-ordered to participate as part of a family reunification plan are motivated to improve their parenting, while others are clearly unmotivated and put forth minimal effort. Similarly, many foster parents we have worked with have been strongly motivated to learn new skills, while others consider treatment participation to be too time-consuming and "beyond the call of duty."

We encourage all of the child's major caregivers to be involved in treatment. In two-parent families, we think it is important that both parents participate. Participation by both parents decreases the chances that one will undermine or "sabotage" treatment, and participation by both increases inter-parent support and childrearing consistency. Many times, one parent is resistant because of beliefs about division of childrearing responsibilities or because of a difficult work schedule. In those cases, we encourage whatever level of participation is possible, and we initiate treatment with the more motivated parent. It is usually the motivated parent who is the child's primary caregiver and in the best position to influence the child therapeutically. On several occasions,

Table 1-2. Factors Influencing the Effectiveness of PCIT

Parent factors	*Child factors*	*Family factors*
	Factors increasing effectiveness	
Average or higher IQ	Age between 2 and 7	Good marital adjustment
Strong motivation	Good receptive language skills	Extended family support
	Factors decreasing effectiveness	
Active substance abuse	Under age 2 or over age 7	Severe marital discord
Severe psychopathology	Pervasive developmental disorder	Extreme family chaos
Mental retardation		
Court-ordered/unmotivated		

we have worked with mothers whose husbands were initially uninterested in participating, saying that the child behaved just fine with them and that misbehavior was only the mother's problem. However, after several sessions, resistant fathers often begin to demonstrate interest in participating or observing therapy sessions as a result of the significant improvements they observe in their children's behavior at home.

PCIT is often ineffective in families with severe marital discord, particularly those characterized by spouse battering. Couples engaged in verbally and physically abusive relationships are generally too chaotic and stressed to put forth the consistent energy necessary to make use of this program. We advise individuals in such relationships to obtain individual and marital counseling and inform them about community resources for keeping themselves and their children safe. For couples whose marital problems are less severe and involve disagreements about childrearing strategies, PCIT may be effective for child problems and may lead to decreases in marital discord (Eyberg & Robinson, 1982).

Severe parental psychopathology, such as major depression and uncontrolled thought disorder, is a contraindicator for PCIT. For individuals with these problems, we recommend a course of individual therapy and an evaluation for the appropriateness of pharmacological treatment prior to beginning PCIT. However, in our clinical experience, we have found that individuals whose mood problems are caused or exacerbated by feelings of parenting inadequacy may experience significant mood improvement as a result of participating in PCIT.

Another parental contraindicator to PCIT is active substance abuse. PCIT emphasizes consistent nurturance and limit setting. In our experience, parents who are actively abusing alcohol or other substances are unable to carry out the intensive and consistent home practice required for PCIT to be successful. For these families, we recommend a drug and alcohol abuse evaluation and follow through on treatment recommendations prior to initiating PCIT. However, parents who are well into their rehabilitation programs may be effective participants in PCIT.

In addition to parents with average and above-average intelligence, we have conducted PCIT with mildly retarded and borderline IQ parents. However, modifications have been necessary to achieve success. Less session time is spent presenting material didactically, with correspondingly more time spent in role-playing and direct skills coaching. As would be expected, more sessions are needed to achieve skill proficiency, and generalization of skills to a variety of settings must be directly programmed. For example, several sessions are needed in naturalistic settings such as the home, the grocery store, the shopping mall, and other public places where child management problems arise. In our experience with these families, skills rapidly deteriorate after treatment is concluded unless frequent booster sessions are held.

PCIT is most effective for two- to seven-year-old children. Children younger than two may benefit from the developmental stimulation that occurs in the behavioral play therapy portion of PCIT, but they do not have sufficient cognitive development to benefit from the discipline component. Although we use PCIT with seven-year-olds, we sometimes find that treatment does not produce the same magnitude of change that we find with younger children. On occasion, we have used PCIT with developmentally delayed eight-year-olds who were not severely aggressive. We generally recommend, however, that more developmentally appropriate treatment approachs (e.g., contingency contracting interventions) be used with children over age seven.

Children with pervasive developmental disorder diagnoses such as autistic disorder are less likely to benefit from PCIT. For autistic children, we recommend using one of the model programs designed specifically for this population. For a description of a variety of model programs for young children with autistic disorder, see Olley, Robbins, and Morelli-Robbins (1993).

We have sometimes been asked by therapists inexperienced in PCIT whether we get bored doing the same therapy over and over again. The answer to that question is that boredom is not an issue: PCIT is never the same for any two families, and treatment is always tailored to the individual needs of the family. Some presenting problems require shifts in treatment emphasis, modification of the basic treatment components, reordering of treatment components, or incorporation of additional components. All parents bring their own personalities and parenting philosophies to treatment, and different therapeutic styles are required to join and work effectively with different families.

DUAL FOCUS ON RELATIONSHIP BUILDING AND BEHAVIOR MANAGEMENT

In many other approaches that evolved from Hanf's two-stage model (e.g., Forehand & McMahon, 1981), the first stage of treatment focuses on teaching parents to use their attention selectively. That is, prosocial behaviors are increased by rewarding them systematically with parental attention, while undesirable behaviors are decreased through ignoring. Although parents are also instructed in selective or "strategic" attention as a part of the behavioral play therapy stage (also referred to as Child Directed Interaction) of PCIT, the focus is more broad and humanistic. A major goal of the first stage of PCIT is to establish a warm, loving relationship between the parent and the child. Parents are helped to recognize their children's many positive qualities, are taught how to respond to their children in a sensitive and genuine fashion, learn how to relate to their children at their level of development, and learn to stimulate their young children's development. Misattributions concerning child misbehavior are identified and reframed, leading to a deescalation of anger in coercive relationships. Improvements in child behavior are expected to come as a result of this deescalation of coerciveness in the parent–child relationship (Patterson, 1982). As they grow to like their children more, parents tend to place fewer demands on them, pay more attention to their children's positive attributes rather than finding fault, and children become genuinely more eager to help and please their parents. In fact, some children with anxiety/depression or mildly oppositional behavior may be effectively treated with the behavioral play therapy component alone, obviating the need for the discipline stage.

However, for most families with noncompliant young children, the second stage of PCIT, which addresses discipline strategies, is necessary for treatment success. In the discipline stage (also referred to as Parent Directed Interaction), parents learn how to give effective directions to their young children, and are instructed in how to provide consistent consequences for behavior. For discipline to be most effective, it must take place in the context of a rewarding parent–child relationship (Campbell, 1990; Dowdney & Pickles, 1991). For this reason, the discipline stage of PCIT has traditionally been introduced only after families have successfully mastered the behavioral play therapy component. However, our research evidence suggests that many parents prefer to begin with the discipline component over the behavioral play therapy component (Eisenstadt, Eyberg, McNeil, Newcomb, & Funderburk, 1993). For children who are extremely aggressive and unable to benefit from the behavioral play therapy component without prior work on behavioral control, we have reversed the sequence of stages and begun with the discipline portion of PCIT. Also, some developmentally delayed children with behavior problems who do not possess even rudimentary play skills benefit most from beginning with the discipline portion. For these children, the discipline stage can easily be directed to focus primarily on teaching learning-readiness skills, and the effectiveness of the subsequent behavioral play therapy component is greatly enhanced. For most children, however, we maintain the traditional stage order and begin with relationship building before progressing to discipline training.

TYPICAL COURSE OF TREATMENT

PCIT always begins with an intake session in which information is gathered on presenting problems, formal testing is conducted, and the therapist observes (and may videotape) a sample of how the parents and child relate to one another. We have found it helpful in some cases to break this session into two briefer sessions conducted at different times and on separate days. Many factors influence how a child and parent act on any given day (e.g., whether the child is hungry, had a nap, or is coming down with a cold, whether the parent has a headache or is fatigued), and the best picture emerges when at least two observations can be collected. However, the desire for collecting multiple observations must be balanced against the realities of managed health care and the urgency many parents feel about getting therapy under way. Conducting too much pretreatment testing leads to unnecessary attrition, particularly for parents who are action-oriented or coping with multiple life stressors.

Feedback regarding assessment results and treatment planning is provided to families either at the end of the first intake appointment or at a separate feedback session. If PCIT is to be recommended, the typical course of treatment is described to the family, emphasizing the ways in which PCIT can address the specific concerns that brought them in for treatment and any additional areas of concern that may have emerged from the evaluation.

As mentioned earlier, treatment usually begins with the behavioral play therapy component. After giving feedback, a teaching session is scheduled in which the therapist meets only with the parents and teaches them the basics of behavioral play therapy using discussion, viewing of videotaped models, live modeling, and role-playing. Parents are not just lectured to; they are active participants who are encouraged to generate numerous questions and consider how the principles discussed fit with their parenting philosophies.

After the teaching session, the parents and child are seen together for several sessions of direct coaching on behavioral play therapy skills. The specific number of sessions needed depends on how rapidly parents are able to acquire the skills and the nature of the child's presenting problems, but we find that most families are ready to move on to the discipline stage after two to four coaching sessions. Predetermined skill criteria are used to assist the therapist and family in deciding when it is time to move ahead to the discipline component of PCIT.

After mastering the behavioral play therapy goals, the therapist again meets alone with the parents for a session to teach them the basics of the discipline stage of treatment. This teaching session is also highly interactive, consisting primarily of role-playing and problem-solving. Again, the parents are seen together with the child for several sessions of direct skills coaching. These sessions begin in the clinic setting and may be extended to community settings to enhance cross-setting generalization. Treatment is usually concluded when all of the presenting problems have been resolved or substantially improved. We find that most families meet their treatment goals after approximately four to six discipline sessions.

A posttreatment evaluation session is held in which the measures that were administered before therapy are repeated, and videotaped observations of posttreatment parent–child interactions are conducted. To streamline the post-treatment evaluation, we sometimes videotape parent–child interactions at the end of the last discipline coaching session and send parent-report measures home to be completed and returned to us prior to the posttreatment feedback. Feedback involves reviewing the pretreatment to posttreatment changes on formal measures as well as in the videotaped interactions of the family. This session helps parents to solidify their recognition of improvements that have been occurring gradually over several weeks of treatment. For most families, the full course of

Table 1-3. Steps in Parent–Child Interaction Therapy

Step 1: Pretreatment assessment of child & family functioning and feedback (1 to 2 sessions)
Step 2: Teaching behavioral play therapy skills (1 session)
Step 3: Coaching behavioral play therapy skills (2 to 4 sessions)
Step 4: Teaching discipline skills (1 session)
Step 5: Coaching discipline skills (4 to 6 sessions)
Step 6: Posttreatment assessment of child & family functioning and feedback (1 to 2 sessions)
Step 7: Boosters (as needed)

treatment can be conducted in 8 to 12 sessions (see Table 1-3), and is consistent with the short-term treatment philosophy adhered to by many health maintenance organizations. Booster sessions are usually held at 1, 3, 6, and 12 months to enhance maintenance of parenting skills and to address problems that arise as children face new developmental challenges.

OUTCOME RESEARCH

In programmatic work examining the effectiveness of PCIT, Eyberg and her colleagues have demonstrated statistically and clinically significant improvements in child disruptive behavior and noncompliance (Eyberg & Robinson, 1982). Using clinic-based training, treatment effects have been found to generalize to the home (Boggs, 1990) and to untreated siblings (Eyberg & Robinson, 1982). In addition, PCIT with individual families has been shown to be more effective than parent group didactic training (Eyberg & Matarazzo, 1980). In a sample of families with a high proportion on welfare (35%) and many single mothers (55%), we found significant improvements not only in oppositional child behaviors, but on parent-report of activity level, parenting stress, child internalizing problems, and child self-esteem (Eisenstadt [Hembree-Kigin]*et al.,* 1993). Clinically significant improvements were maintained at one- and two-year follow-up evaluations (Newcomb, Eyberg, Funderburk, Eisenstadt [Hembree-Kigin], & McNeil, 1990), with no significant differences found in outcome for families who began with the behavioral play therapy versus those who began with the discipline stage of PCIT. Also we have described how the behavioral play therapy portion of PCIT is useful for stimulating language skills in developmentally delayed preschoolers (McElreath & Eisenstadt [Hembree-Kigin], 1994).

While several research groups have found that children's school behavior worsens as a result of clinic- and home-based parent training, the opposite has been found with PCIT. The positive effects of PCIT have been shown to generalize to the day-care, preschool, and early elementary classroom settings in the absence of any direct classroom intervention. We compared conduct-problem young children to both normal and disruptive classroom control children before and after completing 14 weeks of PCIT in the clinic (McNeil, Eyberg, Eisenstadt [Hembree-Kigin], Newcomb, & Funderburk, 1991). Treated children showed clinically significant improvements in direct observation and teacher-report measures of noncompliance and disruptive behavior at school. The specific behaviors that improved included disobeying teacher directions, talking back, teasing, hitting, talking out of turn, whining, yelling, and breaking school rules. However, significant improvements were not found in hyperactivity and inattention in the classroom and in peer relationship problems. A follow-up study of these children indicated that classroom improvements were maintained for the year following treatment and, to a significant but lesser extent, at the 18-month follow-up (Funderburk, Eyberg, Newcomb, McNeil, & Eisenstadt [Hembree-Kigin], 1990).

In an uncontrolled study of at-risk children, we evaluated the effectiveness of PCIT conducted in foster parent workshops and found significant pre- to post-workshop improvements in child behavior problems as well as a high degree of participant satisfaction (Clemens-Mowrer, McNeil, & Armstrong, 1992). A controlled outcome study was recently completed documenting the effectiveness of PCIT delivered in a culturally sensitive Head Start workshop for parents of at-risk African-American children (Lipson & Eisenstadt [Hembree-Kigin], 1993). In addition, a large-scale demonstration project of PCIT is currently under way at the University of Florida (Eyberg, 1994).

In summary, the overall effectiveness of PCIT is well-documented. There is no doubt that groups of children and families improve dramatically as a result of this intervention. Yet, as clinical researchers, we also are aware of families who have been less successful. Like any treatment program, PCIT has its strengths and limitations. We hope this book will help clinicians determine which families are most likely to benefit from the standard PCIT package. Helpful tips also will be offered for modifying PCIT for those difficult and complex cases that inevitably find their way onto caseloads.

The First Session

With new case referrals, we always begin PCIT with an evaluation of child and family functioning. We think this is important for several reasons. First, PCIT is not a "cookbook" approach to child treatment in which therapy procedures are the same with all families regardless of presenting problems. Instead, the particular emphasis and treatment components are tailored to meet the special needs of each family, and the way that we learn about those special needs is through our initial evaluation. The initial evaluation can also elucidate factors that may interfere with treatment progress so that they can be addressed prior to or concurrent with PCIT.

The second reason we begin with an evaluation is that the results of our testing serve as a baseline measure of child behavior and parenting skills against which we judge the family's progress during the course of treatment. We collect information in every coaching session on how well the parent is implementing the specific skills we are working on, as well as on how well they are maintaining the skills taught previously. If we do not see substantial improvements over our baseline measures, it is a "red flag" for us to stop and assess why treatment is not progressing as expected. Sometimes adjustments need to be made in our teaching strategies. At other times, we find that we missed a key piece of information about family functioning at the time of our initial evaluation and that this particular factor (e.g., substance abuse, severe parental depression) is interfering with treatment progress.

The third reason we believe it is important to begin with an evaluation is accountability. Clinical judgments concerning treatment effectiveness, no matter how strongly held, are subject to many biases and should not be the exclusive source of information about treatment results. Also, in this climate of managed health care, mental health professionals will increasingly be expected to objectively document the effectiveness of services rendered in order to obtain third-party reimbursement.

JOINING WITH PARENTS

We approach every PCIT evaluation with the expectation that we will be working with this family in treatment; we want to make the assessment process an experience that enhances therapeutic rapport. Although we recommend a core battery of assessment procedures, we often supplement this battery with additional measures or reduce the assessment procedures as needed. For some families, particularly those who are well-educated and "psychologically minded," a lengthy evaluation that is thorough and detailed will enhance rapport as well as provide a great deal of helpful information. The enhanced rapport is likely to translate into greater acceptance of treatment recommendations and better follow-through on practice at home. For other families, particularly those that are highly stressed and looking for rapid results, a lengthy evaluation may be interpreted as "bureaucratic red tape" and a lack of responsivity to the family's needs. Highly stressed families and those that are distrustful of mental health professionals are likely to drop out of therapy if the initial evaluation is too lengthy and contains elements that do not appear directly relevant to their situation. For all families, we look for an immediate and salient service we can provide in the initial evaluation session. Sometimes we help them to apply for social security income benefits for a developmentally delayed child, advocate on their behalf with the school system, or request transportation from local community services.

FLEXIBLE BATTERY APPROACH

We recommend using the core set of assessment procedures outlined in Table 2-1. However, we adhere to a flexible battery approach in which we supplement these procedures with additional measures of child, parent, and family functioning depending on the needs of the individual family. Table 2-2 presents a list of several of the supplementary procedures we commonly use. Less often, we omit elements of the core battery (e.g., Parenting Stress Index, Child Behavior Checklist), particularly when the parent's reading ability is limited. Most often, we mail a packet of forms for both parents to complete (Child Behavior Checklist, Eyberg Child Behavior Inventory, Parenting Stress Index) and a form to be completed by the child's teacher (Sutter–Eyberg Student Behavior

Table 2-1. Parent–Child Interaction Therapy Core Assessment Procedures

Semistructured intake interview	(approx. 45 minutes)
Child Behavior Checklist—Parent Form	(20 minutes)
Eyberg Child Behavior Inventory	(5–10 minutes)
Sutter–Eyberg Student Behavior Inventory	(if child is in school; 5–10 minutes)
Parenting Stress Index	(25 minutes)
Dyadic Parent–Child Interaction Coding System Observation	(30 minutes per parent)

Table 2-2. Supplemental Assessment Procedures

Parent-report measures
  Social Skills Rating System (Gresham & Elliott, 1990)
  Conners Parent Rating Scale (Conners, 1989; Goyette, Conners, & Ulrich, 1978)
  Vineland Adaptive Behavior Scales (Sparrow, Balla, & Cicchetti, 1984)
  Childhood Autism Rating Scale (Schopler, Reichler, & Renner, 1986)
  Minnesota Multiphasic Personality Inventory—2 (Butcher, Dahlstrom, Graham, Tellegen, & Kraemer, 1989)
  Beck Depression Inventory (Beck, Ward, Mendelson, Mock, & Erbaugh, 1961)
Child-report measures
  Harter Pictorial Scale of Perceived Competence and Social Acceptance for Young Children (Harter & Pike, 1984)
  Peabody Picture Vocabulary Test—Revised (Dunn & Dunn, 1981)
Teacher-report measures
  Child Behavior Checklist (Achenbach, 1991, 1992)
  Social Skills Rating System (Gresham & Elliott, 1990)
  Conners Teacher Rating Scale (Conners, 1989; Goyette, Conners, & Ulrich, 1978)

Inventory) prior to the evaluation session. Having the forms completed in advance shortens the length of time needed for the clinic session, a particularly important consideration with very young children. In a two-parent family, the intake evaluation session can be completed in under two hours.

SEMISTRUCTURED INTAKE INTERVIEW

Our evaluation begins with a semistructured intake interview in which we listen to parents' concerns, collect information about the child's developmental history, inquire about the history of specific problems and strategies parents have used to address these problems, and discuss family stressors. In two-parent families, we set the expectation for equal involvement by both parents and prompt the less vocal member of the pair to share his or her observations and concerns.

We prefer to allow the child to play in the room during the interview. This procedure enables the therapist to get to know the child better by observing the child's play and behavior. Parents are told that the therapist will be watching to determine how well the child responds to the parents' instructions. As such, parents are encouraged to correct and manage their children's behavior in the clinic just as they would in the home setting. It is helpful to tell children the order of events and let them know that the purpose of the session is to learn more about their behavior, school activities, and interests. The therapist should periodically share positive observations about the child during the interview to reduce any negative feelings. In addition, parents are advised before the beginning of the interview that any sensitive information may be shared later in the session, when the child is out of the room. Accommodations can be made for parents who prefer that the entire interview take place outside of their child's presence.

Before beginning the interview, the limits of confidentiality are provided. This is a sensitive issue for many of our clients, given that parents of young children with behavior problems are at risk for losing control of their tempers during disciplining. Also, we often work with families who already are in the child welfare system because of abuse and neglect. We find it helpful to talk about the issues in the third person, so as to distance the abuse question from that particular parent. Emphasis is placed on the confidentiality of information provided by parents. However, an exception is any case in which a child appears to be in danger. To decrease parental defensiveness, an example is given of a case in which most parents would agree that the therapist should report:

> As I'm sure you understand, if one of my child clients came in with bruises or broken bones and told me that his mother had hit him with a board, I would have a legal and ethical responsibility to bypass confidentiality rules to help keep that child safe. Everything, except for a situation in which a child appears to be in danger, is kept private. So, I want you to feel comfortable talking to me about sensitive topics. For example, a common concern of many parents is that they feel that they are losing it with their children. This is a good place to talk about controlling anger and keeping children safe. I am a therapist. That means that I'm here to provide support. Particularly, I'm here to help parents and children get along better. Any questions about all of that?

During the course of the interview, we collect detailed information concerning the family's experiences using time-out. Most families referred to us for disruptive child behavior have used time-out and found it ineffective. On inquiry, we can nearly always identify problems in the way they were using time-out which compromised its effectiveness. It is important to collect this information up front during the intake interview; when time-out is later introduced as a discipline method, the therapist will thus be able to reassure parents that the new form of time-out is different from the unsuccessful one they used previously. A variety of semistructured interview formats are available that are suitable for use in PCIT. We use one that is similar in format to the one published by Barkley (1990, pp. 262–277).

PARENT-REPORT MEASURES

Both parents are asked to complete the Child Behavior Checklist (CBCL; Achenbach, 1991, 1992) as a broad screening measure for a variety of externalizing (e.g., disruptive, acting-out) and internalizing (e.g., anxious, depressed) problems. The CBCL now includes a form for 2- and 3-year-old children as well as 4- to 18-year-olds. The CBCL is a psychometrically sound instrument that we find useful for documenting pretreatment to posttreatment changes following participation in PCIT. The CBCL may be ordered from University Associates in Psychiatry, 1 South Prospect Street, Burlington, VT 05401-3456 (802-656-8313).

The Eyberg Child Behavior Inventory (ECBI; Eyberg, 1974) is an empirically validated, brief parent-report measure of child behavior problems that is appropriate for use with children age two and older. The Intensity Score provides an estimate of how frequently the child displays each of 36 problem behaviors, and the Problem Score allows the parent to rate whether or not he or she perceives the behavior to be "a problem" for the child in question. Children are considered to be rated within the "conduct problem range" when they receive Intensity Scores greater than 127 and/or Problem Scores greater than 11. In our experience, the ECBI is the measure that is most responsive to PCIT treatment effects and should be included in addition to the CBCL if a goal of evaluation is to document the effectiveness of therapy.

The ECBI is particularly useful for identifying parents who may have inappropriately high or inappropriately low expectations concerning their children's behavior. For example, one mother we worked with reported that she considered 20 of 36 behaviors to be problems. However, the frequency with which the child displayed these behaviors was well within normal limits, suggesting that this mother may have had little tolerance for the normal but sometimes irritating behaviors displayed by young children. In contrast, we worked with an overly tolerant father who reported that his son frequently engaged in a large number of disruptive behaviors, but he indicated that he considered none of them to be problems. He expressed the attitude that "boys will be boys," and he felt that his wife and his son's preschool teacher were overreacting to his son's disruptive behavior. The Problem Score tends to be higher in single-parent versus two-parent families, and high Problem Scores have been associated with marital distress (Eyberg, 1992a). The ECBI has been reprinted in the Appendix and can be photocopied for clinical and research use.

The third parent-report measure that is included in our core battery is the Parenting Stress Index (PSI; Abidin, 1990). The PSI may be used with parents of children three months through ten years of age and provides information on temperament-related child behaviors, the parent–child relationship, parent characteristics related to parenting, family context variables, and stressful life events. This measure helps us identify families in which the combination of high parenting stress and significant child behavior problems places the child at risk for experiencing abusive parenting practices. A high score on the marital distress subscale may be a "red flag" for families that would benefit from marital counseling prior to or concurrent with PCIT. Similarly, a high score on the depression subscale may prompt the therapist to more carefully evaluate the extent of parental depression. The PSI is available from Psychology Press, 39 Pearl Street, Brandon, VT 05733-1007 (802-247-8312).

TEACHER-REPORT MEASURE

The format of the Sutter–Eyberg Student Behavior Inventory (SESBI; Sutter & Eyberg, 1984) is similar to that of the ECBI. However, the items have been adjusted to be more appropriate for the classroom setting and the measure is completed by the child's day-care, preschool, or elementary school teacher. Intensity Scores greater than 147 and Problem Scores greater than 14 are suggestive of significant conduct problems (Funderburk & Eyberg, 1989). The SESBI distinguishes between preschoolers referred for school behavior problems and nonreferred preschoolers, and has been found to be sensitive to improvements in school behavior following PCIT. The teachers we work with especially appreciate the brevity of the SESBI, as it can be completed in approximately five minutes. The SESBI is reprinted in the Appendix and can be photocopied for clinical and research use.

PARENT–CHILD INTERACTION OBSERVATIONS

One of the fundamental elements of our pretreatment evaluation is direct observation of parent–child interactions. We conduct informal observations in which we note how the dyad interacts in the waiting area and while parents complete assessment procedures. In our informal observation we look for the child's ability to play independently, strategies the child uses to engage the parent's attention, parental responsivity to child overtures, parental limit-setting, warmth of parent–child interactions, and evidence of clinging and separation anxiety.

Children sometimes become quite disruptive during the informal observations. Therapists should avoid the temptation to intervene, unless of course there is imminent danger. As the child has not yet received treatment, the therapist's attempts to get the child to mind or calm down are unlikely to be effective. Instead, the therapist would probably appear incompetent to the parents, who probably would perceive that the therapist has no better control over the child than anyone else. The best approach is to instruct the parents to manage the behavior as best they can. For example, if the child runs out of the door, the therapist should ask the parents to retrieve him or her. If the child is throwing toys, the therapist should indicate concern and ask the parents to try to stop the throwing. When parents ask for advice, the therapist can support their desire to learn, but help them to realize that the skills are complex. Their questions will be answered in future sessions if they can be patient for a little while longer.

More formally, we conduct a structured observation using the Dyadic Parent–child Interaction Coding System (DPICS; Eyberg & Robinson, 1983).

The observation is done in a clinic playroom using a small table, chairs, toybox, and three to five constructional toys (e.g., Duplos, Lincoln Logs, Tinkertoys, Mr. Potato Head, building blocks, puzzles, toy farms).

Although it is acceptable to conduct the observation with the therapist-examiner observing from within the playroom, we find it preferable to use a childproofed playroom equipped with a two-way mirror, standard intercom system, and a bug-in-ear microphone device. The bug-in-ear allows the therapist to deliver instructions to the parent from the adjoining observation room via an unobtrusive hearing-aid-type device. [The bug-in-ear is available from Mind Works, Inc. (previously Farrall Instruments) P.O. Box 745, Gulf Breeze, FL 32562 (904-934-1142).] We find that young children are much more likely to display the behaviors that initiated the referral if the therapist is out of the room and the children are asked to do things that they might not want to do.

If observing from within the playroom, we suggest explaining to the child:

> My job is just to sit and watch you and your mom (dad) play.
> Sometimes I might write something down, but I can't talk to you,
> not even a little. Your job is to play with your mom (dad) and
> pretend like I'm not even here, like I'm invisible.

In order to avoid becoming a participant in the interaction, the therapist-evaluator must completely ignore any of the child's overtures. After a minute or so, nearly all children will begin ignoring the unresponsive therapist and will interact exclusively with the parent.

During the initial evaluation, we usually do not invite a parent into the observation room to observe their spouse's interactions with the child. Witnessing their spouse's behavior may cause the parent to alter his or her own behavior later when being observed, decreasing the validity of the observation. Also, many couples are initially uncomfortable observing one another and feel self-conscious knowing their spouse is behind the mirror.

Regardless of who is in the observation room, most parents feel nervous about the observations initially. It helps to anticipate this anxiety, reassuring parents that "most people feel a little nervous about this at first, but just try to relax and play with (child's name) like you would at home." Most two- and three-year-olds will be unaware that they are being observed unless they are given an opportunity to see into the playroom from behind the mirror. However, older children who are not developmentally delayed usually realize they are being observed. To diffuse curiosity, we often bring the older child into the observation room briefly prior to the formal observation. We find that once the play observation is begun, children quickly forget that they are being observed as they become engrossed with the play activity. It is also helpful to show curious children the bug-in-ear device. We usually hold the hearing aid up to their ears and are honest about the fact that we will use this to talk to their parents about ways to play with them. Children also are instructed that the hearing aid is not a toy and can break easily. As such, they will not be permitted to play with it.

We recommend that the pretreatment observation be videotaped (with written parental consent and child assent). Videotaping allows for the interactions to be reviewed multiple times, especially important for therapists who are inexperienced in observing parent–child interactions. We save the videotape and make it part of our review of treatment progress at the conclusion of therapy. To ensure that the playroom lights stay on during the videotaping, switches can be protected by mounted lock boxes or hidden by electrical tape. We recommend testing audio levels on the recording prior to conducting the observation.

We observe the parent and child interacting in each of three standard five-minute DPICS situations that vary in the degree of parent control required: *Child Directed Interaction* (CDI), *Parent Directed Interaction* (PDI), and *Cleanup*. The exact instructions given to parents are reprinted in Table 2-3. The *CDI situation*, in which the child is allowed to play with whatever he or she chooses and has the parent's undivided attention, usually brings out the child's most positive behavior and allows the examiner to see how the parent and child relate to one another under optimal conditions. The *PDI situation*, in which the parent picks the activity and asks the child to play along, is more challenging for both the child with behavior problems and the parent. It provides an opportunity to see what strategies the parent uses to engage the child's cooperation, how the child responds to parental directions, and what particular disruptive and noncompliant behaviors the child exhibits. The *Cleanup situation* is the most challenging of all, and if the child has significant behavior problems, they often are displayed during this final situation. Often, the cleanup is not completed within the five-minute observation period. If the child has begun the cleanup, we typically allow the parent to continue to enforce the cleanup

---

Table 2-3. Dyadic Parent–Child Interaction Coding System Instructions for Parents

Child Directed Interaction (5 minutes)
  "In this situation, tell (child's name) that he/she may play whatever he/she chooses. Let him/her pick any activity he/she wants. You just follow his/her lead and play along with him/her."
Parent Directed Interaction (5 minutes)
  "That was fine. Now we'll switch to another situation. Tell (child's name) that it's your turn to pick the game. You can pick any activity. Keep him/her playing with you according to your rules."
Cleanup (5 minutes)
  "That was fine. Now I'd like you to tell (child's name) that it is time to leave and the toys must be put away. Tell him/her that you want him/her to put the toys away. Make sure you have him/her put them away without your help. Have him/her put them away in the big toybox."

instructions. However, with some defiant young children the interaction becomes a standoff and we recommend ending the interaction so as to avoid an escalation in parental anger and potential embarrassment. Occasionally, an otherwise defiant child will clean up quickly, before the five minutes is completed. In such cases, the therapist can prorate the behavioral ratings over the remainder of the five-minute period. To enhance the likelihood of getting a full five-minute observation interval for Cleanup, the therapist may choose to empty three or four toys from their containers prior to the beginning of the DPICS observation.

During each of these three five-minute segments, we keep track of a number of child and parent behaviors and verbalizations using tally marks on a coding sheet. The original DPICS coding protocol provides space for recording 24 parent and child behaviors and verbalizations. However, in clinical practice, fewer of these categories may be recorded to reduce complexity and some categories may be combined. In the Appendix, we have provided definitions of the major coding categories along with a clinically modified DPICS recording form appropriate for use in clinical practice. For research protocols, we recommend using the original DPICS in its entirety or the new and significantly expanded version, DPICS-II (Eyberg, Bessmer, Newcomb, Edwards, & Robinson, 1994).

The behavior we see in a clinic observation may or may not approximate the parent's and child's behaviors in other settings. Following the observation, we ask parents to estimate how typical the child's behaviors were in each of the three situations. Many times, parents will tell us that the child was on his or her best behavior and we did not see how bad things really are at home. Very rarely will a parent indicate that the child behaved worse than is usual at home. In order to maximize the chances of collecting a representative sample of behavior, we may ask parents to bring the child back for a brief second visit in which the videotaped observations are repeated, preferably at a different time of day than the first observation.

CLASSROOM OBSERVATIONS

If the child is enrolled in day care, preschool, or early elementary school, we strongly recommend conducting a classroom observation. Particularly if there are questions concerning attentional problems and hyperactivity, clinic-based observations do not present a full picture and should not unduly influence diagnostic, placement, or treatment decisions. A young child in a one-on-one situation with an adult is often much calmer, more attentive, and more compliant than is typical in the classroom setting. Classroom observations are highly recommended as they provide the best picture of the child's deficits, place teacher observations in context, and yield invaluable information for forming treatment recommendations.

The best information is obtained when children are observed at different times of day, on multiple days, and during a variety of activities that vary in their demand for rule-governed behavior (individual seat work, circle time, and free play provide a good range of behavior to observe). We find it useful to ask the teacher to point out three children to observe: the referred child, a child who has average behavior for the classroom (but not a model of excellent behavior), and the child whose behavior most closely approximates that of the referred child (see McNeil *et al.*, 1991). Observing the average child provides a marker for what is normative behavior in that classroom, and observation of the child whose behavior most closely approximates that of the target child allows the examiner to determine how much more disruptive the referred child is than the next most difficult to manage child. To maximize the chances that children will be compared while engaging in tasks with similar demands, each is observed for very brief periods (ten seconds) in rotation, with intermittent brief rest periods for marking child behavior and making notes. This method may be used to produce information about the percentage of the observation period in which the target and comparison children were on-task, compliant, and did not engage in disruptive behavior. A similar procedure is described by Barkley (1990, p. 338).

SHARING TEST RESULTS WITH PARENTS

At the end of the intake evaluation session, we meet alone with the parents for approximately 30 minutes to answer questions and provide preliminary feedback on the results of testing. Although we may not have all of the formal measures scored and interpreted, we often have sufficient information from the interview, behavioral observations, and Eyberg Child Behavior Inventory to determine whether we will be able to provide a helpful service for the family. We believe it is important for the family to leave the initial evaluation session feeling that their concerns have been listened to and validated, and knowing that we are ready to provide them with a well-researched service that directly addresses their concerns.

During a separate formal feedback session, we go over the results of testing in detail and share our impressions of the child's behavioral and emotional development. We ask parents to share with us their ideas about why their child is experiencing problems. Often, parents will express guilt and wonder aloud whether there was something they should have done differently during the pregnancy or during early childrearing. In most circumstances, we are unable to precisely determine what factors are responsible for the child's problems. We explain to parents that young children's problems are multiply determined, and it is nearly impossible to say that any one factor caused the problems. However, we emphasize that even though the parents are probably not directly responsible for the development of their young child's behavioral or emotional problems, they are the only people with the power to successfully resolve them. Our goal is to diminish nonproductive guilt, while giving parents back the responsibility for treating their children, thus enhancing their motivation to work hard in PCIT.

This process of reducing parental guilt while encouraging responsibility is a tricky one because the therapist must always be nonjudgmental. If parents think that the therapist views their parenting as "bad" or "inadequate," they will "yes, but. . ." the therapist throughout the skills training. Yet, the therapist is advising the parents to undergo parent training, which to many parents implies inadequacy. One way to deal with this problem is to explain the notion of "specialized parenting." We explain to parents that some children are temperamentally more difficult to parent than others because of short attention spans, difficulty handling change, willfulness, or developmental problems. While typical parenting is usually effective for children with easy dispositions, other children have special needs. Rather than viewing PCIT as a remedial program for dysfunctional parents, we then can view it as a mechanism for helping parents to form a better fit with their children. This "fitting process" involves teaching highly specialized skills that enable parents to manage children who do not seem to respond well to "typical parenting." Clearly, the "specialized parenting" approach is not appropriate for all cases (e.g., parents who over-pathologize their children, abusive parents). Another approach for rapport building is to praise parents for positive parenting skills they displayed during the evaluation. Even when parents demonstrate few positive skills, the therapist can always praise them for caring enough to get help for their child.

If we suspect that the child has a significant developmental delay, we conduct supplementary developmental testing and always schedule a separate, more lengthy feedback session to cover the results of both behavioral and developmental assessment. For thorough and sensitive guidelines for providing parents with feedback concerning their children's developmental problems, we strongly recommend the work of Shea (1984, 1993).

INTRODUCING PCIT TO PARENTS AND CHILDREN

After sharing with parents the results of testing and answering their questions concerning the causes and expected course of behavioral and emotional problems, we introduce them to PCIT. The goal of this introduction is to get parents excited and hopeful about treatment, and to establish the expectation that PCIT will require an intensive effort on their part. We explain that we offer a service that was designed specifically for young children with problems similar to the ones displayed by their child. We then provide an overview of PCIT with brief rationales for the importance of both the behavioral play therapy (Child Directed Interaction) and the discipline (Parent Directed Interaction) components.

We tell parents that if they work hard and their child responds the way many children with similar problems do, we can expect significant improvements in cooperative behavior, happier mood, more affectionate interactions, and improved behavior in the classroom. Depending on what we believe will be most meaningful to a given set of parents, we may support these expectations by citing our clinical experience or the positive findings of our PCIT research studies.

If the parents indicate that they would like to participate in PCIT, we bring the child back into the room and provide him or her with a developmentally appropriate explanation about treatment. For example, for an oppositional four-year-old boy, we might use the following explanation:

> Sometimes you get mad at your mom and dad, and sometimes they get mad at you. I'm somebody that helps moms and dads learn how to play better with their boys. I also help little boys learn how to mind their mommies and daddies better. From now on, you'll get to come here with your mom and dad each week. You'll play with my fun toys while you learn to get along better with your mom and dad. Does that sound OK to you? What toy should I have out for you when you come to play next time?

Teaching Behavioral Play Therapy Skills to Parents

After the initial PCIT evaluation and feedback have been completed, parents are asked to attend a "teaching" session in which the therapist introduces the family to the basic skills of behavioral play therapy. Because a great deal of information is shared and it is important to have the parents' undivided attention, we request that parents arrange for child care during this session. Most often, the teaching session lasts approximately 90 minutes to allow for the many questions that arise in response to the material presented (see Table 3-1).

OVERVIEW OF TEACHING SESSION

The session begins with a description of the goals of this part of PCIT, emphasizing how behavioral play therapy may help resolve the specific problems that were identified during the intake evaluation. Parents are told that they should not worry about taking notes or trying to memorize material because they will be given a handout at the end of the session including all of the information. The rationale for use of brief daily home "play therapy" sessions is described. Next, the therapist presents a set of "Do" skills and a set of "Don't" skills. Each skill is described along with its rationale, examples are given, and the skill is briefly demonstrated by the therapist. The best teaching sessions are interactive, with the therapist inviting the parents to comment on how they think the skills could help their child, how they believe their child will respond, and any problems they foresee. Because relationship-building is an important goal of this part of treatment, *both* parents should conduct daily home play therapy sessions with their child.

By the end of the presentation, we want parents to be able to name all of the "Do" and "Don't" skills, so we use a repetitive teaching style in which we summarize all of the previously presented skills before moving on to the next skill. A mnemonic aid regarding the "Do" skills is the acronym "D-R-I-P," representing each of the "Do" skills (i.e., **D**escribe, **R**eflect, **I**mitate, and **P**raise).

Table 3-1.   Steps for Teaching Behavioral Play Therapy Skills

Step 1	Describe goals of behavioral play therapy	<5 minutes
Step 2	Discuss five minutes of daily home practice	<5 minutes
Step 3	Present and model the "Don't" skills	15 minutes
Step 4	Present and model the "Do" skills	20 minutes
Step 5	Discuss use of strategic attention	15 minutes
Step 6	Discuss use of selective ignoring	15 minutes
Step 7	Model all skills in combination	2 minutes
Step 8	Coach parents as they role-play skills	5 minutes
Step 9	Discuss logistics of play therapy at home	15 minutes

Note. Times are approximate and will vary among families.

After covering all of the "Don't" and "Do" skills, the therapist presents the concepts of "strategic attention" and "selective ignoring" for shaping behavior. The therapist then models using all of the skills in combination, often with the parent or a co-therapist playing the part of the child. Finally, parents are invited to role-play with the therapist providing some gentle in-the-room coaching.

At the end of the session, parents are given a handout summarizing the behavioral play therapy skills and their rationales (see Appendix). We save the handout for the end of the session so that parents are not distracted by reading ahead. In addition to the skills handout, parents are given a "homework sheet" (see Appendix) on which to record their daily practice and any problems that come up so they can be addressed in the next session.

We are sometimes asked by parents if it would be okay to audiotape the teaching session so they can listen to it again at home. There are several advantages to audiotaping. First, it is good to have an audiotape available when there is a reluctant spouse at home who may be convinced to listen. Second, many people learn better through auditory than visual channels, and their retention of the information is enhanced if they can review it on audiotape one or more times. And third, sometimes we work with parents with reading difficulties who are able to make better use of an audiotape than a written handout.

PRESENTING THE GOALS OF "SPECIAL PLAYTIME"

There are many possible goals for behavioral play therapy, and the goals that are emphasized for any particular family should be based on the presenting problems identified during the intake evaluation. We find that behavioral play therapy often improves children's self-esteem, improves the parent–child relationship, helps children to attend longer to play activities, makes oppositional children less angry, and improves frustration tolerance and perfectionism. Behavioral play therapy may be tailored for children with developmental problems, foster and adopted children, children with internalizing problems, and abuse survivors. It is important to convey that special playtime is a therapeutic intervention. If parents perceive this as "just playing," they will discount the importance of this portion of PCIT, and will display only minimal compliance with homework.

EXPLAINING THE FIVE MINUTES OF "HOMEWORK" EACH DAY

The skills presented in this chapter are to be used by parents in a daily five-minute "special playtime" at home. Five minutes may seem brief, but it offers several advantages. First, the brief amount of time removes much of the resistance to home practice that comes with longer practice periods. Parents cannot in good conscience tell us that there are not five minutes available in their busy schedules each day to devote to their young children. Second, by using a brief practice period, parents are able to sustain a high degree of quality during their special playtime, making them less likely to just "go through the motions." Third, although five minutes does not sound like much time, it is perceived as a long time by novice "play therapists" who are concentrating hard on using their skills correctly. Longer practice periods early in therapy can lead to fatigue and diminished enthusiasm for treatment. Finally, a major reason why behavioral play therapy is child-directed is to set up a situation in which the child is most likely to display prosocial behaviors. For children who have behavioral problems, the longer the play session, the more likely it is that their good behavior will deteriorate, detracting from parent–child relationship-building.

We explain the five-minute home sessions to parents by saying,

> The rules that I will be describing are to be used during a daily five-minute special play period at home. I certainly don't expect that you or anyone would be able to keep up this high-quality, condensed therapeutic time for extended periods each day. In fact, I find that parents who try to spend longer than the five minutes actually burn-out on play therapy because it takes so much energy. I don't want that to happen to you. So, the key to making play therapy work is to do a little bit consistently every day, rather than doing it irregularly but for longer periods.

Because we emphasize the use of a five-minute play session, some parents become overly focused on preventing themselves from running overtime. Some even ask us if they should set a kitchen timer to go off at the end of playtime. We discourage such rigid adherence to time rules because it is distracting to both the parent and the child, and detracts from the naturalness and pleasure of the playtime. Furthermore, ending the session abruptly at five minutes may prematurely cut off an activity that the child has worked hard on, causing unnecessary frustration. Instead, we encourage parents to look for a natural breaking point after about five minutes, even if playtime is extended by two or three minutes. At the end of the playtime, parents are encouraged to praise their child for the positive qualities they observed during the session and to express their own pleasure in having shared the time together.

As power struggles can easily develop around the issue of putting the toys away, we encourage parents to handle cleanup in one of two ways: (1) to say, "I'm going to pick up the toys now. You can help if you want," or (2) to allow the child to continue playing by saying, "Special playtime is over now. You can continue playing with the toys if you want. But, I have to do some other things right now." Therapists can help parents accept these nonconfrontive suggestions for picking up the toys by reminding them that cleanup strategies will be covered extensively in the discipline part of the program.

It is important to make it clear to parents from the beginning that play therapy should not be viewed as a "privilege" that is contingent on good behavior from the child. Highly stressed and/or punitive families have a tendency to withhold play therapy when they have had a difficult day with their child, unless this point is addressed directly in the teaching session. We emphasize that special playtime is actually more important on days when the child has displayed a great deal of misbehavior. On those days, the play therapy can help to interrupt the negative cycle by allowing the parent and child to have a very warm and positive time together.

CHILD-DIRECTED PLAY

Parents are told that the overriding rule of behavioral play therapy is to allow the child to lead the activity. We explain to parents that children are at their best when they get to choose the activity, and we want them to get a great deal of high-quality attention while they are behaving well. We also point out that there are few naturally occurring opportunities for young children to be in the lead. All day long children are told what to do by adults, and they are often perceived as the least capable members of their families. Having a brief period of time each day in which they get to be the ones who are most knowledgeable about the activity and make most of the decisions helps to relieve some of the frustrations inherent in early struggles for autonomy. The "Don't" and "Do" skills of behavioral play therapy are presented in Table 3-2.

Table 3-2. The "Don't" and "Do" Skills of Behavioral Play Therapy

Don't give commands or make requests
Don't ask questions
Don't criticize or correct in a negative way
Do **D**escribe appropriate behavior
Do **R**eflect appropriate verbalizations
Do **I**mitate appropriate play
Do **P**raise prosocial behavior

TEACHING THE "DON'T" SKILLS OF BEHAVIORAL PLAY THERAPY

The first "Don't" is "Don't Give Commands." Commands take the lead away from the child and set the stage for unpleasantness if the child disobeys. We talk about two specific categories of commands: Direct and Indirect. Direct commands are obvious requests made of the child, such as: "Hand me that crayon," "Sit on your chair," and "Ask nicely." Indirect commands are less obvious and many parents use them without realizing they are subtle forms of commands. Examples of indirect commands include: "How about using the pink now?," "You might want to sit down to do that," and "Could you sing me a song?" These indirect requests take the lead away from the child and should be avoided during play therapy.

The second "Don't" is perhaps the hardest of all of the behavioral play therapy skills to learn: "Don't Ask Questions." Questions direct the conversation instead of following, and tend to take the lead away from the child. Many questions are indirect commands in disguise, and asking questions can also lead the child to believe that the parent is not really paying attention or disagrees with what the child is doing. For example, "Wouldn't you rather play with Mr. Potato Head?" is a leading question implying that the parent thinks the child should play with a particular toy and suggesting disapproval of the child's original choice.

Questions may begin with an interrogative such as "who," "what," "when," "why," "where," or "how," or they may be statements made into questions by the inflection in the parent's voice, for example, "You want to put that there?" (voice rising at end of statement). Many parents have particular difficulty eliminating the voice inflection questions because they do not recognize the subtle changes in inflection. It can help to briefly model and have parents rehearse various statements alternating a declarative versus an interrogative inflection to maximize the contrast.

In explaining the rationale for avoiding questions during special playtime, we tell parents the following:

> Adults ask children far too many questions. If you were to go to a shopping mall, and eavesdrop on conversations adults are having with children, you'll see that almost 75% of what an adult says to a child comes out in question form. Adults ask so many questions because they want children to talk with them. Unfortunately, excessive questioning usually has the opposite effect. Imagine what it would be like if you were constantly bombarded with questions. After a while, you would probably start to feel interrogated and would just give very brief, perhaps one-word responses. Many parents complain that when they ask their children questions about their school day, they get brief, uninformative answers. Often this is caused by a pattern of excessive questioning from early childhood.

Of course, there are times throughout the day when it is important for parents to ask questions of their young children. However, we discourage excessive questioning and discourage all questions during the five minutes of special playtime. We tell parents that in a few minutes, we will talk with them about a much more effective strategy for encouraging their child to talk with them.

The third "Don't" skill is "Don't Criticize." There are several reasons why criticism is discouraged during behavioral play therapy (as well as in all parent–child interactions). First, criticism is not effective for decreasing problem behaviors, and it may even increase some undesirable behaviors. We explain to parents that nearly all young children strive for attention from adults. While they would prefer positive attention, they will work for negative attention if they do not know how to get positive attention. For example, we explain that criticism for talking out-of-turn can actually increase rather than decrease children's disruptiveness. A second reason to avoid criticism is that it causes unpleasantness during the interaction and we want special playtime to be enjoyable for both the child and the parent. The third and most important reason for parents to avoid criticism is that it may result in self-esteem problems. We explain that,

> Young children do not have the cognitive development to be able to reason critically and independently. Their attitudes and beliefs are heavily influenced by the things that adults tell them, particularly statements made by trusted adults like parents. If a parent tells a preschool child that horses fly then as far as the child is concerned, horses *do* fly. Most preschoolers do not have the ability to hear this statement, think back on what a horse looks like, realize that wings are needed to fly, recognize that horses have no wings, and come to the conclusion that their trusted parent has made an error. Similarly, if a parent tells a preschool girl she is dumb, then the girl incorporates that information into her self-image without scrutiny. She does not have the cognitive sophistication to think back to earlier in the day when she was successful at putting together a difficult ten-piece puzzle and realize that the parent is wrong and that she is pretty smart after all.

We consider criticism to be any negative or contradictory statement about the child or what the child is doing. Some criticisms are blatant and uttered only during times of considerable parent consternation. Examples of blatantly critical remarks include "That was a dumb thing to do," "Don't act like such a jerk," and "You sure are ugly when you whine like that." Few parents we work with admit to saying such things to their children, yet we have observed them making these comments when embarrassed by their child's disruptive behavior in the waiting area before or after a session. Thus, even when parents assure us that they do not criticize their children, we still feel it is important to give examples of blatant criticism and to discuss its ill effects.

Another form of criticism that we ask parents to avoid during special playtime is the use of "Don't." Phrases beginning with "Don't" are typically negatively stated commands and take the lead away from the child. Inherent in a negative command is disapproval of the child's activity or behavior. We know that negative commands do not work well with young children who are oppositional, and strategies for managing difficult behavior during behavioral play therapy will be addressed later in this session.

Negative correction is a more subtle form of criticism that nearly all parents use. A negative correction occurs when the child makes an error and the parent points out the mistake before offering corrective information. For example, a child may color the dog purple and say "I'm gonna make him blue." A negative correction would be "That's not blue. You're making him purple." The first three words in this parental response are subtly critical and serve no purpose other than to call attention to the child's mistake. Instead, we encourage parents to leave off the first part, while retaining the noncritical second part of the correction. In this way, parents are able to teach their young children during special playtime without leading or criticizing.

TEACHING THE "DO" SKILLS OF BEHAVIORAL PLAY THERAPY

After presenting all of these "Don't" skills, parents are often left wondering what is left for them to say and do during special playtime. We assure them that there is plenty! The first "Do" skill is "Do Describe." Parents are encouraged to watch their child's activity closely and to comment on even miniscule aspects of the child's appropriate play. Description is a form of attention that is very rewarding to young children, and undesirable behaviors such as mild destructiveness and throwing toys should obviously not be described.

We employ the analogy of a sportscaster broadcasting a play-by-play description of a game. For example, as a child assembles Mr. Potato Head, the parent might say, "You're looking at all the pieces and trying to decide which one you want. Oh, you decided to put a green cowboy hat on Mr. Potato Head. Now he has a mustache. You picked the green glasses that match the green hat (child struggles to put them on). Those glasses are tough to put on, but you're trying really hard. I'll help you if you want me to."

Descriptive statements provide several benefits. First, if a parent is describing the child's activity, the child is always kept in the lead. That way, the child has opportunities to come up with his or her own ideas, to problem-solve with minimal intervention, and is not rushed to keep pace with the parent. Second, continuous descriptions are a clear demonstration that the child has the parent's undivided attention. The child does not need to whine or bang toys on the table to get a response from the parent. Undivided attention can be self-esteem building in that it communicates that the parent thinks the child's choice of activity is interesting. Third, descriptions can be used as a teaching tool for preacademic or early elementary school concepts. For example, parents can count aloud small numbers of blocks, or observe that the green tree in the child's picture matches the green frog on the child's shirt. The parent can make observations about the sizes and shapes of toys and describe sorting activities. Descriptions can also be used to model and correct grammar and phonological processes. Simple descriptions of child-centered activities are particularly important for stimulating language development in young children.

A final benefit of descriptions is that they help to organize young children's thoughts about play, increasing the length of time they are able to attend to the task at hand. During a running commentary, the child's attention is much less likely to wander because each statement made by the parent maintains the child's focus on the activity. We observe that during behavioral play therapy, young children make fewer switches between toys, and they are more likely to persist and problem-solve in the face of a challenge. We have also observed that after several weeks of consistent behavioral play therapy, these young children often describe their playmates' activities during interactive play, and describe aloud their own activities during solitary play. Over time, these vocalizations diminish and we believe that children internalize this running commentary as "private speech" so that they continue to do a silent play-by-play, assisting themselves in maintaining their focus.

The second "Do" skill is "Do Reflect." By reflect, we mean that the parent should repeat back the basic message of what the child has said, a form of verbal imitation. The message can be extended, elaborated on, or subtly corrected through reflection. For example, if the child says "I builded a house," the parent might respond with any of the following: "You built a house" (grammar correction), "You built a house with a front door" (grammar correction with elaboration), or "You built a green and blue house" (grammar correction with elaboration of preacademic concept). Parents may also use reflections to gently correct phonological process errors such as omitting the last consonant sound of a word (saying "mow" for "mouse"), devoicing consonants (saying /p/ for /b/), stopping consonants (saying /t/ for /th/), and omitting unstressed syllables (saying "ghetti" for spaghetti).

Initially, many parents are able only to "parrot back" the exact content of the child's message, without elaboration. Although these literal reflections sound less natural than elaborative reflections, they are still beneficial, particularly for very young preschoolers. Children between the ages of five and seven will often express puzzlement when parents first begin to reflect their verbalizations. However, most adapt quickly as parents become more skillful at elaborating and extending reflective communications.

Reflections communicate acceptance and understanding and let the child know that the parent is really listening. Adults often get into the pattern of acknowledging young children's statements with a head nod or nondescript verbalization such as "Uh-huh," while their attention is clearly elsewhere. While it may not be practical for parents to give their children their undivided attention on demand throughout the day, parental attention should be clearly communicated during behavioral play therapy. Acknowledgments such as "Yeah," "I see," "Uh-huh," and "How about that" should be replaced with reflective statements clearly communicating understanding of the child's message. In teaching parents to reflect, we encourage them to be aware of times when their child repeats phrases such as "Mommy, look at my star. Do you see my star? Here's a star I made." Repetition can be a signal to parents that the child wants a reflection.

Reflective statements also keep the child in the lead during conversation, encouraging the child to elaborate on topics that are child-centered. As mentioned earlier, the most effective verbal stimulation for young children comes in the context of an ongoing activity of interest to the child. Reflection allows the parent to provide an immediate reward for the child's verbal initiations, encouraging the child to speak more and more often. Reflections are much more effective for encouraging children to speak than are questions, and we ask parents to reflect nearly all appropriate verbalizations the child makes during special playtime.

The third "Do" skill is "Do Imitate." It is important that parents be active participants in the play activity, and not just passive onlookers. By imitating the child, the parent demonstrates that he or she is paying attention to the child's activity and thinks it is interesting enough to do also. Imitation is indeed the sincerest form of flattery, and being imitated by powerful grown-ups is a self-esteem boost to young children. Imitation of the child also enhances the child's imitation of the parent (Roberts, 1979), and forms the basis for one of the most important social skills for young children, turn-taking. Parents should keep in mind that any behavior they imitate is likely to be repeated by the child and to increase. Therefore, good judgment should be used in selecting appropriate child behaviors to imitate.

By imitation, we mean that the parent should play with the same or a similar toy and attempt to manipulate the toy in a way that approximates what the child is doing. We do not mean for the parent to imitate in a literal sense, with every action and every block color perfectly replicated. Basic imitation is a form of parallel play in which the parent approximates the child's activity, always a step or two behind, but keeps the focus of attention on the child's play. For example, if the child is building a tower with the blocks, the parent should also build a tower, making sure to keep it shorter and perhaps less well balanced than the child's tower. The parent may occasionally draw the child's attention to the imitation by saying "Yours looks great. I want to try and build mine like yours." However, the parent should continue to keep his or her attention primarily on the child's activity, maintaining the running commentary.

Imitation is very useful for parents who are not accustomed to playing in a developmentally appropriate way with young children. It removes the burden of thinking up an engaging activity that is appropriate for their child's developmental level. Instead, the child teaches them how to play at the appropriate level. Some perfectionistic and high-achieving parents have difficulty with imitation. Some lose sight of the goals of imitation and have a tendency to want to create the "Taj Mahal" rather than a modest structure that is within their child's developmental capability. We have found this more often in fathers who are accustomed to playing the role of builder and toy assembler/repairer at home. Thus, we caution parents to be sure that it is their child who comes up with the novel, creative ideas during play and to be sure that their "replication" does not appear more attractive than the child's original. Otherwise, the special playtime rapidly deteriorates, with frustration on the part of the child and a loss of interest in the too-advanced activity.

Depending on the child's level of development, the parallel play that is encouraged through imitation may be shifted toward more interactive play, with the parent placing a block on the child's tower and initiating turn-taking. However, if the child resists interactive play, we encourage the parent to select a different toy and casually manipulate it while continuing to focus on the child's solitary activity. Depending on the goals we have for a particular family, we evaluate whether it is more important to maintain the positive, warm tone of the interaction and avoid attempts at interactive play, or to gradually shape basic social skills. Appropriate shifts from parallel to interactive play are difficult to teach didactically, and we usually reserve this topic for direct coaching sessions.

The fourth "Do" skill is "Do Praise." We encourage parents to provide numerous praises during special playtime, an average of one praise every 20 seconds! Two particular types of praise we discuss are unlabeled (general) and labeled (specific) praise. Unlabeled praises are ones that convey approval or affection without specifying exactly what it is that the parent likes. Examples of unlabeled praises include "Terrific," "Nice job!," "You're so sweet," "I'm proud of you!," and "Good." In contrast, labeled praises tell the child exactly what it is that the parent likes. Unlabeled praises can be converted to labeled praises as follows: "Terrific counting!," "Nice job of playing so quietly," "You're so sweet to share with me," "I'm proud of you for being polite," and "Good choice of colors." While both unlabeled and labeled praises are good for children and add to the warmth of the parent–child relationship, labeled praises are particularly valuable teaching tools. Young children will work hard for praise. Whatever behavior or quality the parent praises is more likely to be displayed by the child in the future. Labeled praises are more efficient than unlabeled praises at conveying to the child exactly what can be said or done to earn praise in the future. We explain to parents that,

Although praise is one of the most powerful tools available for improving young children's behavior, it is equally powerful for improving your child's self-esteem. As explained earlier when we discussed criticism, preschoolers believe what their parents tell them in a very profound way. They do not yet have the cognitive sophistication to reason analytically and reject false information. If a preschool boy consistently hears from his mother that he is smart and a good helper, he is likely to incorporate that information into his self-image. Thinking of himself as a boy who is smart and knows how to do things is likely to make him persist longer in problem-solving efforts and increase his confidence in trying new and difficult tasks. Similarly, thinking of himself as the kind of boy who is a good helper will make him more likely to volunteer to help with tasks at home and at preschool or kindergarten.

Praise comes more easily to some parents than others. Sometimes parents have a difficult time praising their young children because they are not demonstrative people by nature. Such individuals seem to benefit from the direct coaching of how to praise and some parents have told us that learning to praise has benefited them in their other interpersonal relationships. Other parents have difficulty praising their young children because of tensions associated with the coercive nature of the parent–child relationship. Some are so angry with their children that they have difficulty recognizing positive child behaviors and attributes that are praiseworthy. When a "praise-able" behavior is recognized, some parents express the attitude that "He should have been doing that all along. Why should I make a big deal out of it when he's been so bad all day long?" Of course, we help them to understand that it is on these difficult days that their praise is especially important. For these parents, initial praises may sound less than genuine and be given in a begrudging fashion. However, we find that with consistent practice and coaching in behavioral play therapy, the parent learns to focus more and more on the child's positive attributes and praise comes much more naturally.

Praise can be a difficult or awkward skill for some parents because of childrearing beliefs that may be culturally based. For example, in working with Native American families in Oklahoma, we found that many of them were uncomfortable with the intensity and directness of the labeled praises in this program. Out of respect for their cultural beliefs, we modified the behavioral play therapy to include more subtle forms of praise, such as pleasing facial expressions and indirect praises (e.g., "Your grandmother would like that picture"). We also decreased the intensity of positive feedback given to these parents during coaching sessions. Parents from other cultural groups have told us that relatives and friends have expressed disapproval when they have complimented their children in public, saying the children would be spoiled and that the real world does not give out compliments. When parents appear resistant to providing praise, it is essential to acknowledge the resistance and respectfully discuss these attitudes with them before moving forward in treatment.

USING STRATEGIC ATTENTION

Young children's behavior can be effectively shaped through "strategic attention." By strategic attention, we mean using the "Do" skills of play therapy to carefully reward the behaviors or qualities that we would like to see the child display more often. The first step in using strategic attention is to identify those behaviors or qualities that the parent sees as desirable and prosocial, even if the child rarely displays them at first. Often these desirable behaviors become more clear as parents are encouraged to think of the opposite of problematic behaviors. For example, behaviors or qualities that might be targeted include using polite manners, making good eye contact when speaking, smiling, being gentle with the toys, using an indoor voice, persisting at difficult tasks, playing quietly while the adults talk, sharing, and taking turns.

Once these behaviors are identified, the second step in strategic attention is for the parent to be on the lookout for the targeted behavior to occur, trying to "catch the child being good." For example, "Sarah" was a loud child who played roughly with the toys, banging them on the table. Her father learned to look for even the briefest moment when Sarah was holding a toy gently or placed a toy on the table quietly. Immediately when that occurred, we coached him to say something like "You put that toy down so quietly and softly (descriptive statement). I really like it when you treat the toys nicely (labeled praise). I think I'll play gently with the toys just like you do (imitation)." By the end of the clinic behavioral play therapy session, Sarah was working very hard to earn her father's praise for being gentle, and she was playing with the toys with exaggerated care. Her father was able to accomplish this without ever giving her a command or making a critical statement. We encourage parents to use strategic attention whenever possible through the day, not just during behavioral play therapy.

USING SELECTIVE IGNORING

Just as parental attention in the form of descriptions, praise, and imitation can be used strategically, many behaviors can be shaped by withdrawing attention strategically. We call this technique "selective ignoring." As soon as we bring up the technique of ignoring, most parents tell us that they have already tried it and it simply does not work with their child. We explain to them that selective ignoring is an advanced skill that few people use effectively without special training. There is a great deal to know about what problems can be reduced with ignoring, what situations are most appropriate for the skill, and how to ignore effectively. Although we encourage parents to use selective ignoring for particular problems during behavioral play therapy, we make our discussion of the technique more general so that the principles can be applied outside of special playtime.

The first step is for parents to identify child behaviors or qualities that they would like to see diminished; we write these on the chalkboard to aid in further discussion. The types of behaviors often named by parents include whining, talking back, hitting, throwing a tantrum, tearing things up, fighting with siblings, lying, being sad, nagging, and running away in public places. Unfortunately, not all of these problem behaviors can be diminished through the use of ignoring. The first important principle for parents to understand about ignoring is that for it to be effective, the child must be doing the problematic behavior to get a reaction from the parent. We illustrate this concept by saying,

> If you want your son to stop eating a cookie, will it work to turn your back to him and ignore? No, of course not. The reason he is eating the cookie is because it tastes good, not because you are watching him. If your daughter is jumping up and down on the mattress and box springs, will it work just to leave the room? No, of course not. She's probably not jumping up and down just to 'get your goat'; she's probably enjoying the bouncing motion. If your son whines about wanting to go to McDonald's, could it work for you to say 'We don't have time to go today' and then leave the room, ignoring any further whining? Yes it could. Children don't whine because whining is fun all by itself. I've never seen a child sitting alone in a room whining. What makes whining rewarding for young children is the reaction they get from their parents. If you consistently deprive him of that reaction (and your presence) when he whines, his whining should dramatically decrease.

After giving these examples, we go through the list of behaviors that the parents would like to see diminished. The therapist helps the parents to analyze whether or not their attention rewards the child for engaging in each of the behaviors, and whether removal of attention should be expected to impact the behavior. Many of the behaviors the parents listed will not be appropriate targets for selective ignoring, and will need to be addressed later in the discipline portion of PCIT. We erase those from the chalkboard. Most often sibling conflict is not being rewarded by attention from parents, but instead by the negative attention from the sibling. Lying and stealing are not good candidates for ignoring because they are not reinforced by parental attention. Most preschoolers who lie are doing so to avoid getting into trouble for something they have done, and most young children who steal are rewarded simply by having possession of the desired object.

A second important principle for parents to understand about ignoring is that the behavior that is ignored will get worse before it gets better. When a child is accustomed to getting a particular reaction from the parent and one day that reaction does not come, most will respond by escalating to a more disruptive level that has a better chance of getting the parent's attention. In deciding whether a particular problem can be diminished through ignoring, the parent must make a judgment about whether he or she can tolerate having the behavior get worse before it gets better. We ask parents to look back at the list of remaining behaviors on the chalkboard and help them to decide whether they are ones they can tolerate having get worse. It is never a good idea to ignore behaviors that could escalate and potentially be dangerous to the child or to others. For example, playfully running away in public places and physical aggression should not be ignored.

Some parents will feel able to ignore problem behaviors at home such as whining and talking back, even if they escalate. However, they may not feel prepared to ignore these behaviors when they occur in the presence of relatives or in public places. We encourage them to talk with us about why they feel unable to ignore in public settings. Many express the belief that onlookers will scrutinize them and be critical of their parenting if they simply ignore whining and talking back. Often such fears are markedly exaggerated. Later in PCIT, we will work with parents on disciplining their children in public places and it is helpful to identify early any cognitions that may interfere with follow-through on behavior management in public. Some parents tell us that they cannot tolerate having any of their child's problem behaviors get worse before they get better. Such individuals are usually highly stressed and feel considerable anger toward their children. They may not be open to using selective ignoring as a behavior management tool.

The third principle parents must understand to use selective ignoring effectively is that once they begin to ignore a behavior, they must ignore it all the way through to the end. If the parents give in and reward the child with their attention (even if it is negative attention) after the child's behavior has already escalated, they will teach the child that a higher level of disruptiveness will be necessary to have the desired effect in the future. This principle is explained to parents using the "checkout line" example.

> Imagine that while you are waiting in the checkout line at the grocery store, your daughter asks you nicely for a Tootsie-Pop. You tell her 'no' because she has already had enough candy for one day. She responds by whining softly that she wants 'just one, please.' You decide to ignore her whining and pick up a magazine and start thumbing through it. Your daughter reacts by whining more and more loudly, becoming increasingly demanding. You notice that she has gotten the attention of people nearby and you are feeling embarrassed. You tell her in an angry tone 'Be quiet. I told you *no*.' She throws a full-scale temper tantrum and you buy her the Tootsie-Pop to calm her down. What you have accidentally taught her is that asking politely is not the way for her to get what she wants. But, she can get exactly what she wants if she is loud and

obnoxious enough, particularly when you are in a public setting with lots of people around. Next time you take her to the store, you can expect her behavior to escalate even more quickly. How else could this be handled?

Parents are invited to briefly problem-solve with the therapist about alternatives. Parents need to decide right away about whether they are up to ignoring all the way through. For parents who indicate that they cannot or will not ignore throughout, we discuss the principle of "giving in early." It is better to reward the early stage whining than the later-stage tantrum. Given that ignoring is not a strategy for all situations nor for all parents, other discipline strategies are presented later in PCIT.

During behavioral play therapy, most young children are on their best behavior and display only minor problems (e.g., whining, talking back, bossiness, loud voice, rough play with toys). These can be addressed through selective ignoring of problematic behavior with strategic attention paid to incompatible behaviors. The therapist models for parents the use of strategic attention and selective ignoring in rapid succession. When the child (role-played by a parent or co-therapist) is behaving appropriately, the therapist leans toward the child, makes good eye contact, and describes, imitates, reflects, and praises. Particular attention is paid to behaviors that are incompatible with identified problem behaviors such as using a big boy voice, asking politely, using an indoor voice, and playing gently with the toys. As soon as the child begins to whine or talk back, ignoring begins with the therapist turning in the chair to face away from the child. No further eye contact is made, no words are exchanged, facial expression stays blank (even if the child is clowning) and the therapist pretends that the child is not there. However, the therapist unobtrusively watches for the first possible moment when attention can be returned to the child, in other words, when the child pauses or ceases the disruptive behavior. When that happens, the therapist swings back around in the chair, makes eye contact with the child, and says something like "Thank you for playing gently with the toy. It's so much more fun to play when you treat the toys nicely."

Ignoring should never be subtle. We want to maximize the contrast between how the parent responds to the child when the child is behaving appropriately and how the parent responds when the child is disruptive. Exaggerating both the attention and the ignoring will help children to learn prosocial behavior more quickly. Sometimes the child's disruptive behavior is prolonged and it is difficult to find a momentary pause during which to return attention. In those situations, we encourage the parent to "ignore and distract," which involves moving away, playing with a different toy, and enthusiastically describing their own play, but as though talking to oneself. Most often, the child will quickly cease the disruptive behavior to join the parent in the new and attractive activity. The parent then has the opportunity to provide strategic attention for appropriate behavior. Another skill used while ignoring is "modeling the opposite behavior." For example, while ignoring his child who has begun a barnyard brawl with all of the farm animals, the father can begin to enthusiastically describe how much fun his animals are having because they are good friends who play exciting games together. It is not uncommon for the child to begin participating in the more cooperative play being modeled by the parent. The "ignoring" teaches the child what "not to do," and the "modeling" teaches the child what "to do" instead to obtain the father's attention.

HOW TO HANDLE DISRUPTIVE BEHAVIORS THAT CANNOT BE IGNORED

Although unusual, some of the children we work with who have severe behavioral disturbances display a variety of conduct problems that cannot be ignored during behavioral play therapy because they are dangerous to the child or to others. Such behaviors include standing on top of furniture, throwing or breaking toys, hitting or biting the parent, putting small toys in their mouths, and banging on observation room mirrors. These behaviors are more apt to occur during our coaching sessions in the clinic which last up to an hour than during the very brief daily sessions at home. In both settings, we encourage the parent to intervene as needed to ensure the child's and parent's safety. At home, parents respond to aggressive or dangerous behaviors by discontinuing that day's special playtime session and disciplining the child using any safe method of their choosing. For most children, discontinuation of the play session is sufficiently punishing that repeated episodes of aggression during play therapy rarely occur. In the clinic, a brief restraint is sometimes used to protect the child or parent. This involves having the parent hold the child's arms above the wrists for approximately 20 seconds with eyes averted and head turned. In clinic coaching sessions, behavioral play therapy may be resumed immediately or after a short rest break in order not to miss out on valuable coaching time.

MODELING SKILLS IN COMBINATION

While describing each of the behavioral play therapy skills, the therapist briefly demonstrates the skill in isolation. However, this does not give parents an accurate picture of how the skills are used in combination. We have sometimes modeled use of the combined skills with a parent or co-therapist pretending to be the child. At other times, we have used a posttreatment videotape segment of a real parent using the skills with a child who presented with problems similar to those of the referred child, or with a child and parent of similar cultural background (written authorization to use the tape for this purpose is required). Social learning research tells us that modeling is most useful when the parent perceives the model to be similar to him- or herself. We also find the videotape particularly helpful in that we can pause it, make observations, and review the segment again.

ROLE-PLAYING OF BEHAVIORAL PLAY THERAPY

After demonstrating the combined skills, we ask parents to briefly role-play. For single parents, the therapist can ask a co-therapist to play the role of the child, or if a co-therapist is not available, the therapist can do double-duty as both the child and the therapist-coach. In two-parent families, we ask one parent to play the part of the child while the other parent plays him- or herself. Most parents experience some performance anxiety during this first role-play. We try to lessen that anxiety by maintaining a positive, praising tone and interjecting anxiety-defusing humor whenever possible. After getting over their initial anxiety, many parents find this the most enjoyable part of the teaching session.

We recommend doing three brief role-plays of about one minute each. In the first, the child should be perfectly behaved and present no behavior management challenge. In the second, the child should show intermittent minor disruptive behavior but behave appropriately most of the time. In the third, the child should behave much the way that the parent predicts their child will behave. In the case of behavior problem children, most parents significantly overestimate the amount of disruptive behavior their child will display in this situation.

The therapist-coach should encourage parents to begin with describing, and gradually add the other "Do" skills. If the parent is having difficulty getting started, the therapist may suggest specific phrases for the parent to repeat. After nearly every parent verbalization, the therapist-coach should immediately and quietly provide brief feedback such as "nice description," "good reflection," and "good labeled praise." Because they are concentrating hard on their verbalizations, most parents will need to be gently prompted to imitate. It is not necessary to correct every error that the parents make during these role-plays; there will be plenty of opportunities to correct errors during subsequent coaching sessions. The purpose of the role-plays is to introduce the parent to how it feels to do the skills and what it is like to have someone providing them with frequent, largely positive feedback on their performance. The parents should leave the session recognizing that play therapy will be a challenge, but one that is well within their grasp.

APPROPRIATE TOYS FOR BEHAVIORAL PLAY THERAPY

Parents should have a set of three to five toys that are always available for the child to play with during special playtime. Most parents find that their children already have several appropriate toys and they need not purchase new ones. Other parents have found it helpful to purchase two or three inexpensive toys that are put away and brought down only during special playtime. This strategy helps to preserve the novelty of the toys and adds to the child's anticipation of daily special playtime. However, we do not advise parents to restrict the child's access to toys that he or she already possesses, as this would (justifiably) seem unfair and detract from the goal of enhancing the parent–child relationship.

We give parents a handout summarizing the types of toys that are good for behavioral play therapy and those that are to be avoided (see Appendix). In general, constructional toys without preset rules are best. Examples of constructional toys include Duplos (for three- to five-year-olds), Legos (for six- or seven-year-olds), Waffle Blocks, building blocks, Tinkertoys, magnetic blocks, Lincoln Logs, Erector Sets, Mr. Potato Head, magnetic picture boards, crayons and paper, and chalkboards and colored chalk. Sets of plastic figurines and building structures are also appropriate for behavioral play therapy. Examples include farms and stables, doll houses with miniature people, and race tracks or garages with toy cars. All of these toys encourage creativity and provide developmentally appropriate opportunities for problem-solving in the context of play. They are calm, prosocial, sit-down activities that set children up to be on their best behavior.

We caution parents to avoid toys that are conducive to rough play like bats, balls, boxing gloves, and punching bags. With these toys, children who are prone toward behavior problems become overly excited, often requiring parental interventions that take the lead away from the child and cause unpleasantness. Similarly, we encourage parents to avoid toys that set the stage for aggressive play. Such toys would include toy guns, swords, cowboys and Indians, and superhero characters. For very disruptive children, toys that are messy and can get out of hand (such as paints, scissors, and Playdoh) also should be avoided during behavioral play therapy.

Board games and card games with preset rules do not work well in behavioral play therapy. The child may be the loser in the game, have trouble taking turns, or cheat, causing unpleasantness during a time when we want to encourage parent–child bonding, not competition. Although we strongly encourage parents to read to their children daily, we discourage reading during special playtime because it interferes with spontaneous parent–child conversation. Because we want parents and children to talk directly to one another during behavioral play therapy, we advise parents to minimize the use of toys that encourage participants to pretend they are other people, speaking through their pretend characters. Examples of these are puppets, costumes, toy telephones, and dolls.

ISSUES IN ONE-PARENT AND TWO-PARENT FAMILIES

Behavioral play therapy is particularly helpful for one-parent families. When parents are highly stressed and overburdened with the responsibilities of single parenthood, quality playtime with children is rare. Behavioral play therapy provides a practical mechanism by which a single parent can assure spending some individual, high-quality time with the child each day. In fact, our research suggests that children from single-parent families demonstrate larger gains in self-esteem after PCIT than do children from two-parent families (Eisenstadt [Hembree-Kigin], 1990).

In two-parent families, sometimes we are asked whether the parents can alternate days conducting behavioral play therapy. Because one of the goals is to improve the quality of the parent–child relationship, we feel it is important that *each* parent do behavioral play therapy *every day*. Dynamics in the marital relationship often become apparent during behavioral play therapy treatment sessions. Some couples are very supportive of one another and are able to serve as effective "coaches" for each other at home. That is, they can observe one another unobtrusively and offer constructive feedback, much as the therapist-coach will do in treatment sessions. Other couples are highly critical of each other, or have power imbalances such that it is best if they do not critique one another. We share with parents the potential advantages and disadvantages of observing one another and allow them to come to their own decisions about how they will practice.

WHAT ABOUT SIBLINGS?

We suggest that parents also do behavioral play therapy at home with all of the referred child's siblings who are between the ages of two and seven. Children love special playtime. Directing this special attention only to the referred child often causes jealousy in siblings. Moreover, we find that siblings of the referred child often experience clinical or subclinical problems and may benefit from the effects of behavioral play therapy. Parents can usually generalize use of the skills from the referred child to the siblings with little difficulty. Most often, we recommend that parents begin play therapy at home with all of the children, but bring only the referred child for initial practice sessions in the clinic. If the parents are experiencing difficulty adapting their skills to the siblings, we sometimes schedule an extra session of brief coaching with the siblings.

ADJUSTING PLAY THERAPY TO THE CHILD'S DEVELOPMENTAL LEVEL

When parents are doing behavioral play therapy with siblings of the referred child, they sometimes need help adapting the skills to the appropriate developmental level. The skills as described in this chapter are appropriate without modification for four- and five-year-olds. For children who are two and three years old, parents should expect the child to play more comfortably on the floor than at a table. The selection of toys should be adjusted to the toddler age-range, using perhaps stacking rings, soft blocks, toy trucks, and push toys. Hand games like patty-cake may also be used. Toddlers change activities more frequently than do older preschoolers and a sufficient number of toys should be available to maintain the child's interest. Parent verbalizations should be shortened and simplified to provide the most effective stimulation. If the child has few words, any attempts at verbalization or sound-making should be reflected and imitated and praise should be specifically directed at verbal communication attempts. To maintain toddlers' interest, parental affect should be exaggerated, with highly animated praise and even hand-clapping.

For six- and seven-year-olds, we recommend that parents concentrate on a very natural tone, as exaggerated animation and overly enthusiastic praise will sound artificial and condescending. Reflections with older children should never sound "parroted." Instead, they should be highly elaborative without directing the topic of conversation.

PROBLEM-SOLVING WITH PARENTS ON LOGISTICAL ISSUES

Parents need to make decisions about where they will conduct their home play sessions and at what time of day they will occur. Rather than leaving parents to sort these problems out for themselves, we prefer to spend a few minutes assisting them with their problem-solving. Behavioral play therapy should be conducted in a place that is quiet, private, and free of interruptions and distractions. It should not be done in a room with the television playing or with siblings intruding. Nor should it be done in the child's bedroom if there are toys in sight that would be inappropriate for special playtime, but tempting to the child. Many parents find that the kitchen or dining room table works best, while others prefer playing on the floor in the parent's bedroom or a guest room.

We recommend that the play sessions occur at about the same time each day and be incorporated into the family's daily routine. When special playtime occurs at differing times each day, young children often become anxious about missing out on their time with their parents. They can sound like a broken record, continuously nagging the parent to play with them. This situation certainly detracts from the pleasure experienced by both the parent and the child and does not contribute to relationship enhancement. Many parents use special playtime as a way to calm children down before bedtime. We find that bedtime preparations often go more smoothly when children know that special playtime always comes after brushing teeth, putting on pajamas, and so forth.

Some children have difficulty accepting the end of their playtime and try to manipulate the parent into spending extra time. If the parent wishes to extend the interaction, we recommend discontinuing the specific skills of behavioral play therapy and engaging in another activity that is appealing to the child such as playing with dolls or tossing a ball in the backyard. In this way, the child continues to enjoy the parent's company but the parent does not "burn out" on the play therapy skills. Another way to help children accept the end of special playtime is to schedule it at a time immediately preceding another desirable activity such as a favorite television show, snack time, or story time. Most scheduling problems occur in families with two or more young children. If it is a two-parent family, they may choose to take turns providing childcare for one another during play therapy sessions. When only one parent is available, special playtime can often be accommodated by staggering naptimes or bedtimes.

ASSIGNING PLAY THERAPY "HOMEWORK"

Each parent is asked to commit to practicing behavioral play therapy at home with their child for five minutes every day for one week until the next clinic session. They are reminded that they are not expected to become "play therapists" overnight. For the next few sessions, they will be coached in how to use these behavioral play therapy skills. They are given a recording sheet on which to mark whether they got in their practice and to record any problems that came up during the playtime (see Appendix). For many families, this "homework" sheet serves as a reminder to practice, although the children are so fond of their special time that they rarely allow the parent to forget. The homework sheet also helps to make parents feel accountable, as it is reviewed with the therapist at the beginning of the next session.

4

Coaching Behavioral Play Therapy Skills

Novice PCIT therapists can coach the basic behavioral play therapy skills with little or no prior experience. However, coaching is an art that continuously develops as the therapist gains experience working with parents from diverse cultural groups, with various communication styles and disparate childrearing attitudes, and with children who present unique challenges. Although skillful coaching develops from experiences working with dysfunctional parent–child dyads, it is also grounded in a solid understanding of early child development and normative parent–child interactions. We feel it is particularly important for the PCIT therapist to develop and maintain an "internal barometer" for the wide range of interactional styles and communication patterns that characterize healthy, nurturant parent–child relationships. In this way, the therapist will broaden his or her repertoire of coaching strategies and will reduce the tendency to develop professional "myopia," in which similar interactional sequences are coached in all families, without regard to the family's unique communication strengths and style.

There are several ways to develop a barometer for healthy parent–child interactions. We have been able to accomplish this by observing many families in our longitudinal studies on normative parent–child interactions as well as through exposure to the parent–child interactions of friends and relatives. Others we know have made it a point to observe neighborhood parent–child play groups and to spend time in other settings frequented by parents and their young children. Although coaching is enhanced by observing both dysfunctional and adaptive parent–child interactions, skills are acquired most quickly through co-therapy with an experienced coach.

OVERVIEW OF A TYPICAL COACHING SESSION

Table 4–1 presents the different steps involved in typical coaching sessions for families in which one or both parents are participating. Most often, the session begins with the child playing independently while the parent and therapist discuss the child's progress and review the previous week's home practice. After

Table 4–1.   Steps for Conducting a Behavioral Play Therapy Coaching Session

One parent participating
Step 1	Check-in and review of homework	10 minutes
Step 2	Recording of play therapy skills	5 minutes
Step 3	Coaching of play therapy skills	35 minutes
Step 4	Feedback on progress and homework assignment	10 minutes
Step 5	(Optional) Individual time with child	5 to 10 minutes

Two parents participating
Step 1	Check-in and review of homework	10 minutes
Step 2	Recording of first parent's skills	5 minutes
Step 3	Coaching of first parent's skills	15 minutes
Step 4	Recording of second parent's skills	5 minutes
Step 5	Coaching of second parent's skills	15 minutes
Step 6	Feedback to both parents and homework assignment	10 minutes
Step 7	(Optional) Individual time with the child	5 to 10 minutes

this check-in time, we observe the parent conducting a five-minute play therapy session with the child, without doing any direct coaching. Parental use of behavioral play therapy skills during these five minutes is recorded on a clinically modified Dyadic Parent–Child Interaction Coding System (DPICS) recording sheet (see Appendix). After this five-minute observation period, the parent is directly coached by the therapist while continuing to practice the behavioral play therapy skills with the child. For two-parent families, the parent who is not being coached learns through observation. Whether stationed behind a mirror or inside the room, the observing parent should be quiet so as not to interrupt the coaching. The last ten minutes of the session is spent providing parents with feedback on their progress and identifying areas that should receive special focus during the next week's home practice. For five- to seven-year-olds who are particularly angry or distrustful at the beginning of therapy, the therapist may choose to reserve an additional few minutes at the end of each coaching session for individual rapport-building. This individual time can decrease resistance to therapy by encouraging children to view the therapist as an ally rather than as a conspirator with the parents. Although the number of behavioral play therapy coaching sessions will vary based on how quickly parents master the skills, the basic steps outlined in this chapter are used in each coaching session.

SETTING UP FOR THE COACHING SESSION

The parent and child meet with the therapist in a childproofed playroom equipped with a table and chairs and three to five behavioral play therapy toys. Toys that are inappropriate for behavioral play therapy should be removed from the room to avoid the unpleasantness that may occur if the child insists on playing with an inappropriate toy. Because parents will be asked to avoid limit-setting during play therapy, the playroom should contain no items that may inspire the child to misbehave and require parental intervention. In our playroom, we do not include lamps, glass framed pictures, nicely upholstered furniture, sinks, boxes of tissues, or personal items such as handbags. Light switches are kept in the "on" position using lockable covers or tape.

If the therapist will be coaching via a bug-in-ear microphone device, the earpiece should be sterilized with an alcohol wipe and tested prior to the start of the therapy session. Additional materials that will be needed during each session are as follows: one DPICS coding sheet for each parent, one homework sheet for each parent, one skill acquisition recording chart for each parent (see Appendix), a clearly visible wall clock with a second hand or a stopwatch, and sticker rewards for cooperative behavior (optional).

CHECK-IN AND HOMEWORK REVIEW

The session typically begins with the child playing independently nearby while the parent and therapist review the child's home and school adjustment during the previous week, discuss familial stressors, and review the week's homework practice. We ask parents to bring in a homework sheet each week indicating whether or not they were able to practice each day and noting any questions, observations, or concerns they had during the course of the week. Because one of the goals for the behavioral play therapy stage of PCIT is for parents to become more adept at recognizing and praising their child's positive qualities and behaviors, we are careful to prompt parents to note progress and accomplishments by the child, not just problems. We also use this check-in period as an opportunity to teach parents to shape independent play by giving their child intermittent labeled praises for playing quietly while the adults talk.

In order to maximize the amount of time spent in direct coaching of behavioral play therapy, we restrict this initial "check in" to five to ten minutes. Occasionally, the parents we work with have difficulty sticking to this time limit or bring in concerns about important marital or individual issues. If this occurs on a consistent basis, diverting focus away from the parent training intervention and slowing PCIT treatment progress, we recommend inviting parents to participate in adjunctive interventions such as individual treatment, support groups, or marital therapy. Thus, important concurrent issues may be addressed in a planful way, often enhancing the effectiveness of PCIT. With some parents who tend to offer overly lengthy and detailed descriptions of their child's misbehavior, we choose to sequence the session so that this check-in period is saved for the last ten minutes of the session. This limits nonproductive focus on child misbehavior both by decreasing the time available for it and by inviting parents to review child behavior only after they have been coached to focus on their child's positive attributes and behaviors.

During the first behavioral play therapy coaching session, the check-in period should include a brief review of the "Do" and "Don't" skills. Most parents feel quite self-conscious about performing these new skills in front of the therapist. It is helpful to directly address this anxiety, letting parents know that it is a common experience that will quickly pass, and reminding them that the therapist does not expect them to be "masters" of play therapy after practicing it for only one week. Finally, the check-in period during the first behavioral play therapy coaching session should be concluded with a developmentally appropriate explanation of the coaching process for the child. If the therapist-coach will be recording and coaching the skills from an observation room and the child is old enough to perceive that the parent is receiving instructions over the bug-in-ear, the following explanation might be given:

> It's time for me to leave now so you can have special playtime with your mom (dad). But, I'm going to watch you and your mom (dad) play. I'll be watching from behind that mirror. Do you want to see? [Allow child to enter observation room and briefly view the playroom.] I'm going to help your mom (dad) learn to play in a special way. Sometimes I might say things that she (he) will hear in that funny thing in her (his) ear. That thing is not a toy. You can look at it but you can't play with it. Your job is to just play along with your mom (dad) and have fun, OK?

If the therapist-coach will be recording and coaching from within the playroom, the child might be told something like:

> It's time for you to have special playtime with your mom (dad) now. I'm going to stay here and watch you and your mom (dad) play. My job is to help your mom (dad) learn to play with you in a very special way. Sometimes I will watch quietly and write things down, and sometimes I will say some things to your mom (dad). Your job is to keep playing and pretend like I'm not even here, like I'm invisible! That means you don't look at me or talk to me. You just play with your mom (dad) and pretend like I'm not here, OK?

Both of these explanations should be adapted to fit the cognitive and language development of the individual child, and some therapist-coaches may choose to have the parent repeat the explanation in their own words to enhance the child's understanding. If coaching from within the room, some children will have initial difficulty remembering not to interact with the therapist. The first time this occurs, the therapist should remind the child to pretend that the therapist is not there and subsequently the therapist should completely ignore any further overtures from the child. Most children will quickly learn to tune out the therapist's coaching and to attend to the play with the parent. If the therapist continues to respond to the child's overtures, the latter will become more frequent and coaching will be compromised.

The coaching is begun by asking the parents to explain some simple rules to the child. The therapist-coach directs the parents to tell the child:

> We're going to have special playtime now. You can play with any of these toys on the table and I will play with you. There are two rules for special playtime. You have to stay at the table and you have to play gently with the toys. If you leave the table or play roughly with the toys, I will turn around like this (parent demonstrates) and play all by myself. Then, when you come back to the table or play nicely again, I will turn around and we can have fun playing together. I like how you're playing gently now at the table so I can play with you (parent begins play therapy).

─── OBSERVING AND RECORDING BEHAVIORAL PLAY THERAPY SKILLS

As mentioned earlier, we devote a brief period of time at the beginning of each session to recording parental skills progress. This allows us to closely monitor the effectiveness of our previous coaching, provides us with objective information that can be charted and shared with interested parents, and supplies us with information about what skills should receive particular focus during the subsequent coaching.

We get the most accurate picture of how parents are performing their skills at home when we conduct our recording period early in the session, before doing any coaching. If recording is done at the end of the session, after several minutes of skills coaching, nearly all parents are able to perform at a high skill level. However, this performance is artificially enhanced by short-term retention and typically is uncharacteristic of how parents perform independently in home play therapy sessions throughout the week.

We begin the recording period by telling parents:

> I would like for you to go ahead and begin special playtime now. I'll just watch you for a few minutes and make some notes to myself before I jump in and begin coaching, OK? Show me your best play therapy.

We then allow a minute or so to go by so that the parents may warm up and let any initial nervousness subside as they devote their full attention to their child. We begin timing for five minutes and record tally marks in the appropriate boxes on the clinically modified DPICS recording form. At the end of the five minutes, we take a minute or so to make notes about qualitative aspects of the interaction that we would like to address in the coaching or discuss with the parent at the end of the session. We then quickly transfer the data from the recording sheet to the parent's skill acquisition recording chart. This chart makes it easy for the therapist to track the family's week-to-week progress.

The skill progress information we collect also helps us to determine how close the family has come to meeting a predetermined set of criteria for mastery of behavioral play therapy and progressing to the discipline portion of PCIT. The "gold standard" for behavioral play therapy skills established by Eyberg is presented in Table 4–2. Although we hold this out as our ideal, as good clinicians, we do not adhere to it rigidly. For example, many parents have particular difficulty eliminating questions. We would not require a family with good skill acquisition to spend an extra week or more in the play therapy stage of PCIT because one or two questions slipped out during our coding period if other criteria were well-satisfied.

It should be noted that the criteria presented in Table 4–2 were established based on the concept of "overlearning." We know that after treatment is concluded and parents no longer receive weekly coaching, their play therapy skills will backslide. However, if they have overlearned the skills, performing the "Do" skills at a high rate and completely eliminating the "Don'ts," we expect that even after this backsliding has occurred, their skills will still be sufficient to maintain the child's positive behavior, and long-term maintenance of treatment gains will be enhanced. Overlearning also is important because it enhances generalization outside of the playtime. A goal is for the positive parenting skills to become overlearned habits that occur effortlessly throughout the day. For example, when the child tells an elaborate story in the car on the way home from school, we hope that the parent will automatically provide a reflection of the content. Or, when the two children in the family are playing amiably together in the living room, our goal is for the parent to reflexively provide a labeled praise. It is the overpracticing and overlearning of skills during playtime sessions that lead to the spontaneous use of these skills throughout the day.

Table 4–2. Criteria for Mastery of Behavioral Play Therapy Skills during a Five-Minute Play Session

Give 25 to 50 descriptions plus reflections
Reflect nearly all appropriate child verbalizations
Give 15 or more praises, at least 8 of which are labeled praises
Make no critical statements
Give no commands
Ask no questions
Ignore all negative attention-seeking behaviors

━━━━━ COACHING THE "DO" AND "DON'T" SKILLS: TIPS FOR THERAPISTS

Skillful coaching of the parent–child interaction requires that the therapist-coach provide frequent, specific feedback to parents while not disrupting the natural flow of the interaction. That is a tall order for novice therapists who feel awkward sandwiching their comments between parent and child verbalizations. The following general principles are important for effective skills coaching.

━━━━━ Make Coaching Brief and Precise

The best coaching statements contain few words. Full sentences and lengthy explanations interrupt the flow of the interaction and may cause parents to become flustered as they attempt to divide their attention between the therapist-coach and their child. Because every word must count, the language used should be precise rather than general or vague. The coaching statements may take the form of labeled praises, gentle corrections, directives, and observations. Table 4–3 presents examples of commonly used coaching statements in each of these four categories.

━━━━━ Coach after Nearly Every Parent Verbalization

Every verbalization the parent makes provides the therapist-coach with an opportunity to teach, and the more input the parent receives, the faster and better the skills will be learned. Also, by providing feedback after each verbalization, parents learn to pause and wait for therapist input. Coaching will proceed more smoothly when the therapist and parent develop this type of pacing. Providing intensive feedback requires that the therapist think quickly and react with an appropriate labeled praise, gentle correction, observation, or direction. For novice therapists (and even very experienced ones!), this requires intense concentration and sustained effort which can be exhausting. Therapists must resist the inclination to reduce the frequency of their feedback or to coach in a mechanical fashion.

━━━━━ Give More Praise Than Correction

Many parents begin therapy feeling incompetent in their parenting role. It is critical to the success of PCIT that parents feel supported and successful from the outset. For that reason, the therapist-coach must stay in tune with the proportion of praise to correction being provided. Most parents correctly perform many of the skills from the beginning, providing natural opportunities for the therapist-coach to provide a preponderance of labeled praises. If parents are not producing descriptions, reflections, and praises on their own, the therapist should use directives to get the parent to make particular statements,

Table 4-3. Common Behavioral Play Therapy Coaching Statements

Labeled praises

Good imitation.	Nice physical praise.
I like how you're ignoring now.	Good description.
Great job of following his lead.	Good answering his question.
Good encouraging his creativity.	Great teaching!
Nice timing on giving him back your attention.	Terrific enthusiasm!
Nice eye contact.	Nice labeled praise.

Gentle Corrections

Oops, a question!	Sounds a little critical.
Looks like a frown.	Was that a command?
You're getting a little ahead of her now.	Might be better to say. . .
A little leading.	

Directives

Try to label it.	Can you reflect that?
Say "Nice manners!"	More enthusiasm!
Say it again, but drop your voice at the end.	Let's ignore until he does something neutral or positive.
Say "I like it when you use your big girl voice."	Say "It's so much fun to play with you when you're careful with the toys."
What can you praise now?	How about a hug with that praise?
Praise her for sharing.	

Observations

He's enjoying this.	Sounds very genuine.
He's sitting nicely now.	Now he's imitating you.
She wants to please you.	He loves that praise.
He's talking more now because you're reflecting.	She's handling frustration a little better now.
She's staying with it longer because of your descriptions.	There's a big self-esteem smile!
	You see, anything you praise will increase.
That praise is good for her self-esteem.	By saying "I'm sorry" you just set a good example for polite manners.
That's good practice for fine motor skills.	

followed by labeled praises after the statements are made, and observations concerning the child's responses. For example:

> Parent: (watches child build but does not speak)
>
> Therapist: (gives directive) "Say 'Good idea to make a zoo!' "
>
> Parent: "I like that zoo you're building!"
>
> Therapist: (gives labeled praise) "Nice labeled praise. (makes two observations) She really lights up when you praise her. She's working even harder now."

Although it is important to provide feedback as frequently as possible, it is not always wise to correct every mistake the parent makes, particularly early in treatment when errors are frequent. Correcting every mistake, even if done in a gentle way, can tip the scale in the negative direction causing a parent to feel criticized, inept, and discouraged. An alternative to corrections is the use of selective ignoring for incorrect skill use, followed by strategic attention when the skill is used properly. The following is an example:

Parent: "What do you want to do now?"

Therapist: (selectively ignores question)

Parent: "Are you pretending to take the dog for a walk?"

Therapist: (selectively ignores question)

Parent: "Your dog is going for a walk."

Therapist: (provides strategic attention) "Terrific description! You said it as a statement. There was no question in your voice that time."

After the first coaching session, most parents are performing so many skills correctly that nearly every error can be gently corrected while still maintaining the overall positive tone of the coaching.

Coach Easier Skills before Harder Ones

Some of the "Do" and "Don't" skills are generally easier to learn than others, and parents are more likely to feel immediate success if more focus is placed on the easier skills initially. In our experience, describing is typically the easiest of the behavioral play therapy skills, followed by imitating, reflecting, avoiding criticism, and avoiding commands. The skills that appear to be most difficult for parents to master are avoiding questions and giving praise. We believe that eliminating questions is particularly difficult because of the very high rate of questions most parents give young children at baseline. Asking questions is a difficult habit to break. For some parents, praising is difficult because they are not comfortable expressing affection verbally. Others may believe that too much praise will spoil their child or cause him or her to become boastful. Many parents resist praising because they are caught up in a coercive cycle in which they do not want to praise during special playtime if the child has displayed disruptive behavior earlier in the day. Still other parents simply have difficulty identifying their child's positive and praiseworthy qualities and behaviors. Most parents find that praise comes more easily and naturally after they have been practicing play therapy for a couple of weeks and have been coached on praise for one or two sessions. If the parent continues to experience difficulty generating praise, we recommend processing this issue with the parent in detail.

Use Special Exercises for Difficult Skills

When the parent is performing many skills at the desired rate but one skill appears to be lagging well behind, we may interrupt the behavioral play therapy to conduct special exercises in which the parent is encouraged to concentrate on the particular skill. For example, we may tell the parent, "I want to try a little experiment. I want to see how many times in the next minute you can praise Katy, OK? Are you ready? Now begin." During that minute, we stop coaching other skills and count aloud for the parent the number of praises given. For example,

> Good, there's one . . . that's two . . . three . . . now you're really going . . . think of another one . . . four . . . five . . . six . . . time is up. That was fantastic! You gave 6 praises in only one minute when you really concentrated on it. I knew you could do it. If you did just half that many each minute, you would meet our goal of 15 in 5 minutes.

An exercise such as this one provides encouragement and incentive as well as good practice for parents who are struggling with a particular skill. It is often a better strategy than continuing to provide frequent corrective feedback which can become disheartening for the parent. Other exercises that help parents to focus on particular skills include (1) asking parents to reflect everything appropriate the child says in a two-minute time period, (2) asking parents to catch every question they ask and restate it as a description or reflection, (3) asking parents to turn unlabeled praises into labeled praises, and (4) asking parents to practice alternately dropping and raising the inflection of their voices to make a phrase a statement or a question.

Use Observations to Highlight Effects

Often, we find that abstract discussions of how children respond positively and negatively to particular communications from parents are not sufficiently potent teaching tools. Many times, it is not until the parent actually sees it demonstrated during a coaching session that they are able to recognize and strategically alter their communication patterns to elicit desirable child responses.

Therefore, in addition to coaching parental use of "Do" and "Don't" skills, the therapist-coach should comment on the ways in which the child is responding to the parent. For example, if the parent praises the child for putting the red blocks together and then the child reaches for another red block, the therapist-coach may state an observation such as "Your praise is powerful. Whatever you praise him for, he'll probably do again." Similarly, after the parent reflects the child's verbalization and the child speaks again, elaborating on the same topic, the therapist-coach may make an observation such as "You've given him positive attention for talking to you without taking his lead away, so he'll keep the conversation going." Because these observations contain more words and may interrupt the flow of the interaction, they should be used sparingly and strategically. Sometimes we ask parents to take a short break from play therapy and listen to us for extended observations. At other times, we review the observations with the parent at the end of the coaching period.

In addition to making observations concerning the positive responses the child is showing to parental use of "Do" skills, the therapist-coach may also make observations about the child's negative responses to less desirable parental verbalizations and behaviors. For example, if a parent's "imitating" turns into the building of a far more elaborate structure than the one the child is making (despite warnings about this pitfall during the teaching session), the child may be expected to show any of several unfavorable responses: losing interest in the activity and leaving the parent to play with another toy; making negative comments about his or her own ability; or expressing frustration by damaging the parent's structure or becoming bossy. Rather than coaching the parent early in the sequence to tone down the complexity of the building, it is sometimes more instructional to allow the parent to continue and the child to respond unfavorably, and then help the parent to recognize how he or she precipitated this negative child response. In this situation, the therapist-coach might offer an observation such as "He's showing you that your building was too advanced for him and took away his chance to lead the play."

Make Use of Humor

Although coaching and learning behavioral play therapy is hard work for both the therapist-coach and the parent, it need not be an overly serious and formal process. In healthy parent–child interactions, most parents and children relax, laugh, and find humor in their activities and interactions. We find that the session is much more enjoyable for all involved if the therapist makes use of humor for reducing parental performance anxiety and helping to increase the warmth of the parent–child interaction.

Progress from More Directive to Less Directive Coaching

A goal of behavioral play therapy coaching is to empower parents to use the skills autonomously. This can be accomplished by gradually reducing the use of directives and corrections as parents display increased mastery of play therapy skills. For example, in the beginning of a coaching session, the therapist may need to give parents the exact words for labeled praises. As the session progresses, the therapist may only need to provide a brief prompt, such as "How about a praise?" Toward the end of the session, the parent may have developed the ability to generate his or her own praises. When this happens, the sensitive therapist-coach will step back and simply reinforce the parent's good use of praise and provide observations on its effects.

COACHING STRATEGIC ATTENTION AND SELECTIVE IGNORING ————

To maximize the effectiveness of behavioral play therapy, parents must understand the concepts of strategic attention and selective ignoring described in Chapter 3, and be able to implement them in tandem to shape desirable child behaviors. The therapist-coach should look for child behaviors that are prosocial, occur with low frequency, and are appropriate targets to increase through strategic attention. Often these behaviors are naturally incompatible with identified problematic behaviors. For example, a child who is bossy may have "asking politely" as a target of strategic attention. Using the double-pronged approach, bossiness in turn may be identified as a target for decrease through selective ignoring. Examples of problematic behaviors responsive to selective ignoring and their incompatible prosocial behaviors that may be increased through strategic attention are presented in Table 4–4.

When an appropriate target for selective ignoring is presented during the coaching session, the therapist-coach first identifies the problematic behavior, coaches the parent in selective ignoring until the child ceases the problematic behavior, coaches the parent to return attention to the child for positive or neutral behaviors, and coaches the parent to keep an eye out for prosocial behaviors (which are incompatible with the problem behavior) that can be responded to with strategic praise. The following example illustrates the use of selective ignoring and strategic attention in tandem.

Child: "Pow, pow, pow. You're all dead." (mimics shooting Lego people with a Tinkertoy gun he has made)

Therapist (to the parent): "That's aggressive. Now is a good time to begin ignoring. Stop looking at him, quickly turn away, and begin building something of your own with some Tinkertoys. Describe out loud what you are making, but speak as though you're just talking to yourself, not to him."

Table 4–4. Behavioral Targets for Strategic Attention and Selective Ignoring

Strategically Attend to . . .	Selectively Ignore . . .
Polite manners	Bossiness, demandingness
Playing gently with the toys	Banging toy on the table
Staying seated at the table	Leaving seat during play
Using a "big boy (girl)" voice	Whining
Talking softly	Yelling
Driving toy cars safely	Repeatedly wrecking cars
Helping, being nice to toy people	Dropping people on floor
Sharing toys	Grabbing toys away
Building prosocial structures	Making toy guns
Trying even when it is hard	Giving up in frustration

Parent: (turns away from child and picks up wheels) "I think I'm going to build a swamp buggy. Here's one wheel . . ."

Child: (louder this time) "Look mom, I'm killing all of them! Pow, pow."

Therapist: "Great job of ignoring. Don't even look at him. Good describing your own play. Let's see if we can get him interested in what you are doing so he stops the shooting. Be very enthusiastic about your buggy."

Parent: "I'm going to make the coolest, baddest, freshest swamp buggy in the whole world!! It's going to have red wheels. Now I'm going to put a green seat here. I guess I'd better find a driver for my swamp buggy."

Child: "Oh, I know, this Lego-man can drive it! Here, I'll show you."

Therapist: "Perfect! You got his attention away from the aggressive play and now he's playing appropriately with you. Let's give him your full attention now and some strategic praise."

Parent: (turns to face child) "What a great idea to have the Lego-man drive! Thanks for playing nicely with the toys so I can play with you again."

Therapist: "Nice labeled praise."

Parent: "Now you're adding a backseat so more people can ride."

Therapist: "Good describing."

Parent: "I'm really glad you're playing swamp buggy with me. I like this much better than playing with pretend guns."

Therapist: "Excellent strategic praise."

COACHING QUALITATIVE ASPECTS OF THE PARENT–CHILD INTERACTION

Although parents are instructed in a set of "Do" and "Don't" skills for behavioral play therapy, these skills do not encompass all relevant aspects of parent–child interactions or the parent–child relationship. Novice PCIT therapists often focus their coaching exclusively on these "Do" and "Don't" skills, neglecting other qualitative aspects of the interaction. This "tunnel vision" may result in play therapy that meets the letter but not the spirit of the mastery criteria cited earlier in this chapter, and which would not be described by an objective observer as warm, nurturing, or promoting parent–child relationship enhancement. Experienced PCIT therapist-coaches integrate coaching of the core skills with coaching of more qualitative aspects of relationships, including physical closeness and touching, eye contact, vocal qualities, facial expressions, turn-taking, sharing, polite manners, developmentally sensitive teaching, task persistence, and frustration tolerance.

Physical Closeness and Touching

There is no "gold standard" for the optimum amount and type of physical closeness during behavioral play therapy. Healthy parent–child dyads vary widely in the nature and degree of physical closeness and touching exhibited in parent–child interactions. In securely attached parent–child dyads, preschoolers will frequently move from very close physical proximity with their parents (e.g., sitting on parent's lap) to wider and wider exploration of the environment with frequent returns to the security of "home base." However, when the parent is a participant rather than observer of the child's play, such as occurs during behavioral play therapy, most securely attached children will play for extended periods of time within two or three feet of their parents, and parents will intermittently touch their children in an affectionate way.

In our work with less functional parent–child dyads, we have observed anxiously attached, clinging children as well as young children who show unusually little interest in interacting closely with their parents. We have also observed parents who hover over their children, engaging in an excessive degree of controlling physical intervention, as well as those who appear to be uncomfortable with physical affection (e.g., hugs, sitting on lap) expressed by their young children. Thus, depending on the needs of the particular family, the therapist may coach parents to: (1) praise their children for more independent behaviors incompatible with clinging, like sitting in one's own chair, (2) combine verbal praise with physical praise such as stroking the child's hair, offering a hug, patting the child's knee, (3) refrain from "restraining" gestures such as grabbing the child's hand to prevent a response, or (4) move closer to the child who has distanced him- or herself from the parent, praising the child for allowing the parent to join in the game.

Eye Contact, Facial Expressions, and Vocal Qualities

In the dominant Anglo-American culture, it is expected that the listener will make eye contact with the speaker during conversation, and a lack of eye contact may be interpreted as avoidance of emotional contact or poor social skills. Some of the parents we work with have significant social skills deficits or discomfort with emotional exchanges and profit from direct coaching in how to model good eye-contact during behavioral play therapy. Modeling good eye contact is helpful but sometimes insufficient for encouraging young children to improve their own eye-contact patterns. For young children who occasionally make eye contact, parents are coached to praise their children strategically and enthusiastically for good eye contact. When eye contact is a very low base-rate behavior, we coach parents to shape eye contact by lifting a toy that has captured the child's attention to their own eye level while they are speaking, and then strategically praising the child for good eye contact when the parent's and child's eyes meet (e.g., "I like it when you look at me when we're talking").

Sometimes, parents master the mechanics of describing, reflecting, praising, and imitating, but the play therapy takes on a monotonous and boring quality. These parents appear to be "going through the motions" but not to have their hearts in it. On reflection, the therapist may notice that he or she is coaching in a monotone as well. When we first notice this occurring, we exaggerate our own animation, then coach parents to play in a more animated fashion, increasing the enthusiasm in their voices, adding clapping to praises for young preschoolers, and exaggerating facial expressions. As the parents add more animation to their play, we offer observations on its effects such as: "He's looking at your face more and making better eye contact now," "Look at her face beam. Your enthusiasm means a lot to her," and "Now she can really tell you're enjoying this time with her." When a parent does not respond to this coaching by brightening his or her affect, it is sometimes an indicator of depression, substance use, or chronic fatigue. At other times, it is an indicator that the parent is resistant to treatment. When this occurs, we temporarily suspend coaching in order to have a "heart-to-heart" discussion with the parent in which we explore these issues. Sometimes adjunctive interventions for depression or substance abuse are recommended, strategies for stress reduction are presented, and sources of resistance to treatment are identified and addressed.

Turn-Taking, Sharing, and Polite Manners

The "Do" skills of behavioral play therapy, at a basic level, represent social communication skills that people of all ages use in their interpersonal relationships. Research has shown that imitation begets imitation (Roberts, 1979), and when parents describe, imitate, praise, and reflect during behavioral play therapy, their young children in turn imitate these skills. Over time, young children begin spontaneously praising their parents, reflecting parental verbalizations, and describing their own and their parents' play. For many children, we believe these positive social communication skills generalize to sibling and peer interactions as well. Other valuable social skills for young children that are not listed as "Do" skills for behavioral play therapy may be targeted and coached, particularly turn-taking, sharing, and polite manners.

The "Do" skill of imitation presents a natural opportunity to coach turn-taking. As the child performs an action, the parent may be coached to label it as the child's turn and then describe it. Then, as the parent imitates the child's action, the parent may be coached to label their own turn in play and to praise the child for allowing them to take a turn. To clarify for the parent how this sequence of interactions may be helpful to the child, the therapist may add an additional observation such as in the example below:

Child: (puts block on tower)

Therapist: "Now label his turn and describe it."

Parent: "You're taking a turn and putting a blue block on the tower."

Therapist: "Good. Now label your own turn and describe it."

Parent: (picks up another block) "Now I'll take my turn and add another blue block to the tower."

Child: "OK, go ahead mom."

Parent: "Thanks for letting me take my turn! Taking turns is fun."

Therapist: "Good labeled praise."

Child: "Yeah, and we're good at it! Now I get to go, right?"

Therapist: "You've taught him that taking turns can be fun, and if you keep praising him for it, he'll probably do it more when he plays with his sister."

Just as young children can be taught the early social skill of turn-taking during the context of behavioral play therapy, they can be shaped into sharing and using polite manners. Most young children will offer the parent a toy at some point during the course of a play therapy session. We encourage parents to recognize this as sharing and reward the child with enthusiastic strategic praise followed by a parental act of sharing. Similarly, most young children will say "please" or "thank you" at least once during a behavioral play therapy coaching session. Parents are coached to label these verbalizations as good manners, provide strategic praise, and be sure to say "please" and "thank you" as appropriate to the child. For young children who do not spontaneously share or use polite manners, we coach parents to periodically model these early social skills, clearly labeling their own behavior so that the likelihood of imitation by the child is enhanced.

Developmentally Sensitive Teaching

Many parents choose to use behavioral play therapy as a vehicle for developmental stimulation as well as parent–child relationship enhancement. Unfortunately, during our baseline observations of parent–child interactions, it may become apparent that the parent is not well-tuned into the child's developmental capabilities. With preschoolers, parents may overestimate the child's fine motor ability (e.g., building, drawing), grasp of spatial concepts, ability to remember sequentially presented information, and speed of mental processing. They may also underestimate the child's ability to persevere at a difficult task, to pick up after him- or herself, or to select the next item needed while building. This lack of accurate perception of a child's developmental level may become apparent when the parent commands the child to perform a task that he or she is incapable of, impatiently interferes in the child's problem-solving by taking over and completing a task for the child, fails to recognize and praise the child for small increments of developmental advancement, or models inappropriately advanced levels of play. Errors such as these may cause the child to feel bad about his or her own abilities or to lose interest in performing a play task that is too difficult. In addition, the parent's ability to effectively teach is compromised when input is pitched at either too high or too low a level.

To ensure that behavioral play therapy is conducted at the child's level of development, parents are encouraged to adhere to the overriding rule that the child is to remain in the lead. Parents are told that it is at this level that children are most interested in the play activity and most receptive to teaching from parents. The therapist should coach parents to (1) accurately perceive their child's developmental capabilities, (2) recognize the next step that is within the child's reach, and (3) teach the next step through subtle prompting, modeling, and shaping of successive approximations during behavioral play therapy. The following is an example of how a parent may be coached to work at the child's developmental level and stimulate learning:

Child: (draws a rough square on the chalkboard) "I'm drawing a doggy!"

Parent: "He needs a head, body, legs, a tail, a face, and a collar like your doggy, Mattie."

Child: (puts down chalk and studies own shoe)

Therapist: "I'm not sure I could remember to draw all of those parts! She's showing you with her long face that it's too hard for her. Let's back up and work at her developmental level. Point to her drawing and say, "You drew a wonderful doggy's head. I think I'll draw one just like it."

Parent: "I love the doggy's head you drew. I think I'll make one too." (draws another square)

Therapist: "Good start! Lets focus just on the face now. Say something like, 'I'm trying hard to remember what doggies have on their faces.' Try to look puzzled."

Parent: "Hmm, I wonder what doggies have on their faces?"

Child: "I know, eyes!" (hops up and draws eyes)

Parent: "What a great job of making eyes."

Therapist: "Good labeled praise and nice job of keeping her in the lead. Now, how can you help her think of the next thing to add without using a command?"

Parent: "This doggy can see us now because he has eyes. But if we gave him a bone he couldn't eat it."

Child: (giggles) "He needs a mouth! I can draw one."

Therapist: "Excellent job of giving her a hint that was within her developmental capability. Now she's drawn a dog's head with eyes and a mouth. If you keep this up, she'll draw the most detailed dog she's ever made. You've broken it down into small steps so she won't feel frustrated or overwhelmed."

Parent: "I knew you could make a doggy's face if we did just one part at a time. You're a smart girl and a good artist."

Task Persistence and Frustration Tolerance

Many of the children we work with are easily frustrated during play as well as during early academic tasks at school. They may show their frustration by giving up when the activity becomes challenging, becoming destructive with materials, whining, crying, or throwing temper tantrums. Once a child has been identified as having difficulty in this area, several coaching strategies may be used to teach parents how to improve their child's frustration tolerance. It is important to note that in many cases, the parents do not have a high degree of tolerance for frustration themselves. This presents a double-edged sword. The parents may find it more difficult to teach positive coping techniques to their child, but they may also benefit from learning new skills to cope with their own frustration, in turn modeling more appropriate coping skills for their young children.

After mastering basic play therapy skills, parents can be coached to provide strategic praise for task persistence, attempting difficult tasks, and staying calm when experiencing frustration. Yet, some children require a more intensive approach. In such cases, parents are coached to demonstrate a mild degree of frustration with a play activity that is similar to one exhibited earlier by the child. The parent is coached to initially verbalize the frustration, then take a deep breath, count to five, and engage in positive coping statements and simple problem-solving strategies appropriate for the child's level of development. The parent instructs the child that this is something he or she can do too when frustrated and then prompts and rewards the child for engaging in positive coping strategies throughout behavioral play therapy. The following example illustrates how we might coach a parent to facilitate positive coping with frustration:

> Child: (struggles to put stick in wheel, then slams Tinkertoy down) "Stupid thing. It never goes in. I can't do it."
>
> Parent: "They're hard to put together. I'll give it a try too."
>
> Therapist: "Good. Now model some mild frustration."
>
> Parent: (struggles to fit pieces together) "This is so hard to put together."
>
> Therapist: "Nice modeling of frustration. Now put the toy down, take a deep breath, close your eyes, and count to five out loud."
>
> Parent: (takes deep breath and closes eyes) "One, two, three, four, five."
>
> Therapist: "Good relaxing yourself. Now talk about how you feel and model some positive coping statements."
>
> Parent: "There. I took a deep breath and counted to five and now I don't feel so angry. Now I'm ready to try again. I know that if I keep trying I might get them to fit together. (tries to fit pieces together and succeeds this time) Boy, am I proud of myself! I was mad but then I stopped, relaxed, and tried again. That's something you can do when you get mad too."

After the parent has learned how to model these steps for the child, the parent can cue the child to use positive coping in response to frustration at home, providing rewards in the form of praise or tangible reinforcers like happy-face stickers. Children can also be cued to go through this sequence of steps in response to frustration at day care, preschool, and elementary school. However, it must be noted that very young children are rarely able to remember to initiate these coping responses at the appropriate times without direct cuing from a parent or teacher. To be most effective, the cue should come early in the child's frustration reaction, preventing the escalation of frustration to a high level that will inhibit effective coping.

HELPING PARENTS HANDLE AGGRESSIVE AND DESTRUCTIVE CHILD BEHAVIOR

Most children are on their best behavior during behavioral play therapy and are rarely disruptive. After all, they have their parent's undivided attention, are playing with novel toys, and get to be in the lead. However, parents must have a strategy for handling disruptive behavior if it occurs during coaching sessions and during play sessions at home. As mentioned earlier, when children engage in mildly disruptive behavior (e.g., whining, talking back) during behavioral play therapy in either the clinic or the home setting, parents are coached to address these problems using strategic attention and selective ignoring described earlier in this chapter. For more serious behaviors such as physical aggression and destructive behavior during home play sessions, we encourage parents to immediately end the special playtime. However, if aggressive or destructive behavior occurs during a clinic coaching session, we usually do not choose to suspend the behavioral play therapy because doing so will result in lost session time and inhibit treatment progress. Instead, we coach parents to use a brief wrist restraint in which the parents give a briefly stated rule (e.g., "no hurting") and then avert their eyes while gently holding the child's forearms for approximately 20 seconds. At the end of the restraint, the parent is coached to say "I'm going to let you go now. Remember, no more hurting." Then the parent is coached to quickly engage in enthusiastic play therapy in order to draw the child into more prosocial behavior. If the child's aggression escalates further, the therapist may choose to enter the room and provide distraction and assistance as needed.

COACHING SESSIONS WITH SIBLINGS

Most parents are able to extend the play therapy skills to the targeted child's young siblings with little difficulty. However, when children are at different developmental levels, generalization of skills can be enhanced by having one session in which the parent is coached with the referred child and with each of his or her siblings in turn. Usually the referred child feels somewhat proprietary about special playtime in the clinic setting. For this reason, we always include some period of coaching for the referred child, even though the greater focus in this session may be on coaching the parent's use of skills with the siblings.

END OF SESSION DEBRIEFING AND HOMEWORK ASSIGNMENT

We reserve the last ten minutes of each coaching session for providing feedback to parents on their skills progress and discussing the upcoming week's homework. Some high-achieving parents are motivated by viewing a skills summary chart. This is a record of their behavioral play therapy performance during the Child Directed Interaction situation at the baseline evaluation and during each recording period in play therapy coaching sessions. They are able to view their progress from week to week, and once they are approaching the "gold standard" the therapist may share with them the details of the criteria for mastery of behavioral play therapy and progress to the discipline portion of PCIT. Other parents, however, are alienated by progress charts. They may view the charts as too reductionistic and failing to do justice to the complexity of their relationship with their child, or the charts may heighten performance anxiety. Clinical judgment should be used to determine which families may profit from this visual feedback.

Feedback should begin by noting for parents areas of progress in the "Do" and "Don't" skills, child responsiveness to these skills, and improvements in qualitative aspects of the parent–child interaction. It is important that corrective feedback be given as well, highlighting areas needing further work. However, as with the coaching, the therapist must carefully attend to the balance of positive and corrective feedback so that parents leave the session feeling both encouraged by their progress and motivated to work hard in the upcoming week. Between behavioral play therapy coaching sessions, parents are asked to complete a daily five-minute behavioral play therapy session at home, and to record their practice on their homework sheet.

Teaching Discipline Skills to Parents

WHY YOUNG CHILDREN SHOULD MIND THEIR PARENTS

The advantages to parents of gaining behavioral control over their young children are obvious. They will be less frequently embarrassed and inconvenienced by disruptive behavior, they will not have to leave work as frequently in response to difficult behavior at school or day care, they will have an easier time obtaining substitute care, and their day-to-day caregiving responsibilities will be much less stressful. However, as advocates for young children, we are less concerned with making life easier for parents than we are with maximizing the happiness, safety, and developmental potential of their children.

There are several compelling reasons why young children benefit from parental control over their behavior. First, an important part of early socialization is learning how to follow rules. Preschoolers who do not learn how to accept limit-setting by their parents are at risk for poor adjustment in kindergarten and may be retained because of a "lack of behavioral readiness" for promotion to first grade. In order for children to acquire self-discipline, rules must first be externally imposed and enforced. After learning to respond to consistent external limits, young children begin to internalize rules for conduct and to demonstrate rule-governed behavior that will facilitate their classroom adjustment. Second, the ability to obey and follow rules is important for the development of early social skills such as following rules in games and turn-taking. Young children who do not develop these skills as preschoolers are at risk for peer rejection when they enter elementary school, and we know that relative standing within the peer group is highly resistant to change even after social skills deficits are remediated.

Third, parents of young children with behavior problems often find it easier to do self-help tasks for their children rather than "do battle" over simple chores. As a result, it is not unusual for preschoolers with oppositional behavior to show mild to moderate developmental deficits in self-help skills such as dressing and undressing, brushing teeth, using utensils properly, and putting away toys. Fourth, although many parents do not recognize this to be true, young children really do want their parents to be in control. Being able to "run the show" is both attractive and highly anxiety-provoking for young children who depend on their parents for safety and nurturance. Fifth, basic safety concerns dictate that young children learn to follow parental rules and respond rapidly to directions from parents. Some of the impulsive and aggressive young children we have worked with have run away from their parents in crowds, run out into busy streets, slipped out of the house during the night, and set the family home on fire while playing with lighters. And sixth, young children with disruptive behavior and those with developmental problems are at enhanced risk for abuse, particularly when other familial risk factors are present. Thus, we feel it is important that clinicians doing PCIT not lose sight of the fact that the primary goal of the discipline program is to enhance the well-being of young children, and the stress reduction and peace of mind experienced by their parents is viewed as an important bonus.

STRUCTURING THE DISCIPLINE TEACHING SESSION

A great deal of specific information is provided in this session, with approximately two hours required to cover the discipline skills in depth. Parents are instructed to attend without the child to decrease distractions. Although parents are encouraged to ask questions if something is unclear, therapists should not allow themselves to become sidetracked. The series of discipline steps are most understandable when explained chronologically, without jumping ahead. If parents ask questions regarding a step that comes later in the sequence, they should be praised for asking a good question but the answer should be delayed until the earlier steps are understood.

The therapist enters the session with the following materials: (1) toys for demonstration, (2) "Giving Good Directions" handout (see Appendix), (3) discipline flowchart (see Appendix), (4) large doll for role-plays, and (5) play therapy homework sheet. Time-out chairs are set up for role-plays and a wall clock with a second hand is clearly visible in the treatment room. An overview of the steps for the Discipline Teaching Session is provided in Table 5–1.

Table 5–1. Steps for Teaching Discipline Skills

Step 1	Explain use of compliance exercises	5 minutes
Step 2	Discuss how to give effective directions	25 minutes
Step 3	Discuss how to determine if child has obeyed	5 minutes
Step 4	Discuss consequences for obeying	5 minutes
Step 5	Discuss consequences for disobeying	40 minutes
Step 6	Present backups for time-out	30 minutes
Step 7	Coach parents as they role-play discipline skills	10 minutes

IMPORTANCE OF CONSISTENCY, PREDICTABILITY, AND FOLLOW-THROUGH

The session begins with an explanation of the basic premise of the discipline program: "Children who have attentional and behavioral problems need a great deal of structure." Structure is defined in terms of consistency, predictability, and follow-through. These terms are explained to parents using examples and analogies. Consistency, for example, suggests that parents will use these discipline skills the same way on a crisp morning picnic as on a dreary afternoon at the mechanic's garage. And, it suggests that parents will strive to respond to misbehavior the same way when they have a headache as they would if they just found a $20 bill in their rosebushes.

Predictability can be discussed by talking about the "robot" approach to discipline. Because children with behavior problems often find it exciting to push the limits and see how the parent will react, it is most effective to respond in a routine and boring fashion. If children know in advance that consequences are always provided with a neutral, robotic expression using preestablished words, much of the stimulation is removed from the procedure.

The analogy of a "brick wall" versus a "rubber band" is often used in discussing the issue of follow-through. This discipline approach depends on parents learning to "say what they mean and mean what they say." If a child with behavior problems perceives that a parent is flexible about rules or consequences, the limits of the rubber band will be tested until it eventually breaks. Parents are encouraged to establish only a few rules, but to enforce them like a "brick wall."

RATIONALE FOR USE OF "MINDING EXERCISES"

At this point in the session, parents are asked how many times their child misbehaves on a typical Saturday. Parents of children with conduct problems may estimate over 100 incidents of misbehavior for the day. We explain that it would be virtually impossible to have adequate consistency, predictability, and follow-through by attempting to improve all behaviors at once. Given that it took years to develop these disruptive behaviors, it makes sense to provide treatment one step at a time. So, where do you begin?

Rather than viewing their children as engaging in 100 separate problem behaviors, parents are taught to view all misbehavior as falling into two categories: noncompliance and disruptiveness. Noncompliance is defined as refusing "TO DO" what one is told. Disruptiveness is defined as doing things that one is told "NOT TO DO." Given that noncompliance has been found to be the central feature of early conduct disturbance (Loeber & Schmaling, 1985), teaching compliance is the first goal of the discipline plan.

Noncompliance may be viewed as a "bad habit" that the child has learned over time. The child may have developed a "knee jerk" reflex of saying "no" or "wait a minute" when given a command, often regardless of the nature of the instruction itself. The best way to teach compliance is to treat it as a skill that can be learned through practice. Parents are asked how they would teach a young child a new skill such as writing his or her name. Usual responses include working with the child one on one, breaking the task down into smaller parts, and overpracticing. This comparison is used to provide a rationale for minding exercises.

Parents will teach their children to mind by establishing small minding goals along the way. First, children will learn to mind by practicing with "play" commands. Basically, the children will receive praise and the opportunity to continue playing if they follow instructions and a negative consequence if they do not follow instructions. Toys will be placed on the table and children will overpractice minding through the use of simple, nonthreatening tasks such as putting eyes on Mr. Potato Head, placing one block on top of another, and handing things to the parent. By receiving a great deal of enthusiastic praise for these small accomplishments, the child begins to view minding in a more positive light and the habit of defying simple requests is weakened. As small compliance goals are reached, the child is provided with more challenging tasks. These typically involve instructing the child to do things that the child does not want to do (e.g., cleaning up the toys, performing a boring task, transitioning to a less interesting activity). Once compliance has been improved within an exercise format, parents are coached in more "real-life" situations such as getting their children to take their hand for walks and getting them to come in from outside.

GIVING EFFECTIVE INSTRUCTIONS

Given the central role of compliance in the discipline program, teaching parents to give good instructions is quite important. Parents must learn which types of instructions (i.e., commands, directives) are most likely to elicit compliance in oppositional young children. It is explained that children with behavior problems respond differently to instructions than do children with calm and cooperative dispositions. A large portion of the noncompliance problem can be corrected by giving well-phrased directives.

Parents are taught to give good instructions while practicing with the toys that the therapist has brought into the didactic session. This introduces parents to the idea that "play" commands can be effective tools for teaching children to mind. The handout on "Giving Good Directions" (see Appendix) is given to the parents as a visual aid to help them better understand the material both in the clinic and at home. The rules for giving instructions to acting-out young children are discussed with parents as follows:

Make Commands Direct, Not Indirect

Parents are asked to use directives that make it clear that the child is expected to do what the parent has requested. In other words, parents are to tell children what to do instead of asking whether they want to comply. Whereas cooperative children tend to respond quite positively to suggestions such as "Let's clean up now, ok?" or "How about putting on your coat?," defiant children may perceive that the parent is indecisive about whether compliance is required. The child's typical response is to treat the instruction like a rubber band and test the limits. Once the rule is explained to parents, the therapist uses the toys to role-play the types of direct instructions that can be provided during minding exercises, giving the parents plenty of opportunities to practice turning suggestions into directive statements.

State Commands Positively

Parents are asked to tell the child what TO DO, rather than what NOT TO DO. Children are more likely to comply with positively stated instructions, and their self-esteem will improve as they get to do the "right" thing instead of stopping a "bad" behavior. A "don't" command is often like a red flag to an oppositional child, challenging him or her to proceed with the disruptive behavior. Another advantage of positively stated commands is that they save the child the step of having to think of an acceptable activity to do instead. At this point, parents are asked how many times a day their child might be told "don't," "no," "stop," and "quit." Some parents estimate 50 or more. They then are asked about the self-esteem and attitude changes that could occur if only half of those instructions were phrased more positively.

For example, parents are asked to imagine that their daughter "Karen" is sticking a marker in her ear, and they respond by saying, "Don't do that!" The best that Karen can do is to "stop being bad." If, however, they tell Karen TO DO something that is incompatible with the problem behavior, there is a clear difference in tone: "Karen, please draw me a picture with that marker." Now, Karen has the opportunity to actually improve her self-esteem by getting to do the "right" thing. Parents can then be given some negatively stated instructions to turn into positively stated incompatible commands (e.g., "Stop scribbling" can be restated as "Hand me the pen," "Don't climb on that" can be restated as "Please get down," "Quit kicking her" can be restated as "Keep your feet to yourself," "No, I don't want you touching that" can be restated as "Please hold my hand," and "That's not the way we treat our toys" can be restated as "Play gently with the doll"). After much practice, this process of changing negative instructions into positive ones becomes a habit that requires little extra effort.

Make Directives Single Rather Than Compound

Instructions should be provided one at a time, rather than stringing several together. Many preschoolers, particularly those with attentional problems, cannot keep a series of instructions in memory, leading them to respond with either noncompliance or partial compliance. An instruction such as the following would therefore be a setup for failure: "Go in there and wash your hands and then bring me your shoes and socks." One instruction that should be avoided for these reasons is telling the child to "clean up" something. Inherent in the "clean up" instruction is a string of smaller directives. For example, "Clean up your room" typically involves a series like this: "Put your shoes in the closet. Put the pillows back on the bed. Get those Legos back in the box. Place those books back on the shelf." A disruptive young child's idea of what is expected with a "clean up" instruction may be very different from the parent's expectations. As such, parents are encouraged to use a series of smaller commands, particularly when the child is in the early stages of learning to mind. Breaking requests down into smaller units also provides the child with more opportunities to experience the positive consequences of obeying.

Make Commands Specific, Not Vague

Parents are taught to avoid vague instructions such as "Be good," "Come on," and "Straighten up" because the child can easily misinterpret the behaviors expected. Parents are asked to suppose that their child, "Josh," is climbing on top of the bookcase and they respond with a vague, "Be careful, Josh." What is Josh likely to do? Often children will say, "I am being careful, dad." A better instruction would have conveyed to Josh exactly what behavior was desired (e.g., "Josh, please get down"), leaving little room for misunderstanding. A common vague command is the use of the child's name without additional information. For example, Kevin is banging on the table with a plastic hammer and his parent says, "Kevin!" Parents should be encouraged to add the specific instruction to the child's name (e.g., "Kevin, please play quietly with the hammer").

Give Directives in a Neutral Tone of Voice

Yelling is a trap that many parents get into with young children who do not seem to listen to them. Once parents begin to use yelling as the signal that they mean business, oppositional children realize that they can get away with ignoring instructions given in a neutral tone of voice. Parents may find themselves always having to yell to get their child's attention. A goal of the discipline program is for children to learn to respond to directions issued in a normal conversational tone. Neutral tone implies a firm, matter-of-fact approach that contains no trace of yelling or pleading.

Be Polite and Respectful

A good habit for parents to get into is to start most instructions with the word "please." Not only is this respectful and models good manners, but it serves as a discriminative signal to the child that an important directive is going to follow and they should listen carefully. For parents who have a particularly difficult time stating commands directly, the "please" has an added benefit. It is more difficult to turn an instruction into an indirect suggestion when it begins with "please" (i.e., It is awkward to say, "Please would you put the blocks away?," but feels quite natural to say, "Please put the blocks away").

Be Sure Directives Are Developmentally Appropriate

When teaching a child to mind, it is important that both the parent and therapist agree that the child is physically and cognitively capable of following the instruction. For example, suppose an oppositional child is given the instruction, "Please draw a house for mommy." The child responds by saying, "I don't know how. You do it for me." This can be either an oppositional ploy or a valid reaction to being asked to do something that is too difficult. To avoid this common problem and to teach parents about reasonable developmental expectations, the only instructions used for practicing compliance are those that are well within the child's developmental capabilities. Children may be guided in more developmentally challenging tasks through indirect commands, but no consequence will be given for disobeying an indirect command.

Use Gestures

Parents are advised to use gestures when giving instructions. Because many of the young children referred for PCIT have either auditory processing problems, receptive language delays, or attentional deficits, gestures are used to enhance comprehension. When the child does not comply immediately, the parent points so as to clarify the objects or places involved. Gestures are more effective than repeated commands (i.e., "nagging") because they involve much less negative attention and preserve the positive tone of the interaction.

Use Directives Only When Really Necessary

To help parents maintain consistency, directives should be reserved for times when it is important that the child obey (e.g., during minding exercises, when the child has left toys on the kitchen floor). If the parent is not invested in having the child obey a certain instruction, indirect or "question" commands can be used to suggest a possible course of action (e.g., "Would you like to give your aunt a hug?," "Hand me that magazine, ok?"). Compliance with indirect instructions (i.e., suggestions) is optional, but consistent consequences will be provided when the child defies directives. The therapist can use this rule to help parents prioritize the importance of various instructions. In most cases, a goal of the discipline program is to greatly reduce the total number of directives given to children.

Incorporate Choices when Appropriate

Preschoolers often comply more readily when given choices. From a developmental perspective, choices help young children to become autonomous and learn decision-making skills. Yet, giving choices to preschoolers is only effective when the choices are very simple and issued at a developmentally appropriate level. When giving "choice instructions," a good rule of thumb is for parents to try to limit the choices to two equally acceptable behaviors. Examples include: (1) "It's time to get dressed. You can put on either your blue sweatsuit or your Batman sweatsuit" and (2) "Your skates need to be put away. You can either do it now or when the cartoon is over." Oppositional children often refuse both choices, and it is better to stick with the original choices than to reinforce the oppositionality by providing additional options.

Provide a Carefully Timed Explanation

Sometimes (not always) it is appropriate for children to be given explanations for why they should do a requested behavior. These explanations can be important teaching tools for young children, helping them to understand the motives of others and the reasons why things are done in particular ways. However, the key to "reasoning" with young children is to provide a carefully timed, brief explanation, without getting enticed into an argument or lengthy discussion. "Carefully timed" means that the reason should either precede the instruction, or be provided after the child has complied. Ill-timed and better-timed examples of reasoning are as follows:

Ill-timed

Parent: "Please put the crayons back in the box." (direct command)

Child: "Why?"

Parent: "Because our special time is almost over." (ill-timed reason)

Child: "It's not time for it to be over yet."

Parent: "Yes, it is time." (argue) "Now put the crayons away." (repeated command/nagging)

Child: "Why can't we just finish our coloring?"

Parent: "Because it's time to go!" (argue)

Better-timed

Parent: "Our special time is almost over." (reason precedes instruction) "Please put the crayons back in the box." (direct command)

Child: "Why?"

Parent: (gesture: points to crayons and box; explanation already given)

Child: (puts crayons in box) (comply)

Parent: "Thanks for doing what I asked you to do. As I said before, we have to clean up because our special time is almost over." (reason provided after compliance)

When a reason is given between the instruction and compliance, it is a setup for an argument. As is apparent in the first example, the oppositional child has a talent for sidetracking the parent away from the central issue, and ill-timed reasoning is often at the root of negative attention-seeking cycles.

DETERMINING COMPLIANCE

Even when commands are well-stated, it may be difficult to determine whether a child has obeyed. Suppose that the parent points to the red block and says, "Please put the red block in my hand." The parent is asked to list all of the possible ways the child could respond to this instruction. Each response provided by the parent is then categorized as either a "comply" or a "noncomply." In addition to the parent's examples, the following "tough calls" should be discussed:

Doing Something Slightly Different from Parent's Request

It is common for oppositional children to test the limits by providing a response that is slightly different from what was requested. For example, the child may put the green block, not the red block, in the parent's hand. It must be assumed that the child knows which block the parent is referring to for two reasons: (1) only developmentally appropriate instructions are included in minding exercises and (2) the parent pointed to the block to eliminate any ambiguity in the instruction. Therefore, the child's response is considered noncompliance.

Dawdling

An example of dawdling is seen in the child who, given a command, tells the parent to wait until the child has finished his or her present activity. Dawdling is handled with the three-second rule. The parent will count silently, "one-thousand-one, one-thousand-two, one-thousand-three." If the child has not made an attempt to comply by the count of three, it is noncompliance. The three-second rule is used because inattentive young children often forget an instruction if they do not respond to it immediately.

"Playing Deaf"

When a young child ignores a parental request, it is tempting for the parent to repeat the instruction, assuming that the child has not heard it. However, repeating commands provides negative attention to the child and teaches the child that consequences can be delayed or avoided through the use of stalling tactics. Unless there is reason to believe that the child indeed has a hearing problem, it is best to consider "playing deaf" to be a form of noncompliance. In our experience, children quickly learn to attend to instructions if consequences are provided for ignoring parental requests.

Partially Complying

An example of partial compliance is the child who angrily pushes the red block toward the parent without actually placing it in the parent's hand. This is another way in which children test the limits. If the parent accepts this as a comply, the child will view the parent's rules as being elastic. The likely result is that the child will push the limits a little further the next time. The best response is to have the parent silently point to the block and then point to his or her hand to clarify the instruction. If the child does not respond to the visual cue by placing the block in the parent's hand, it is considered noncompliance.

Minding with a Bad Attitude

Imagine that the child slams the red block into the parent's hand and yells, "Here's your stupid block! Now shut up!" Because the child put the block in the parent's hand, this must be considered compliance. After all, the parent did not specify that the child had to put it in the hand gently. Parents are instructed to praise the compliance and ignore the bad attitude. Because the bad attitude is not rewarded with parental attention, we find that it rapidly diminishes.

Undoing

"Undoing" occurs when a child initially obeys and then behaves in a way that negates the obedience. For example, a child may place the red block in the parent's hand and then quickly remove the block. In the original instruction, the parent said to put the block in his or her hand, not to put the block in the hand and leave it there. Although the child is clearly testing the limits, this is considered compliance. If "undoing" continues, the parent can be coached to follow immediately with a second instruction that is more clearly stated such as "Please put the block back in my hand and leave it there."

RATIONALE FOR DISCIPLINING CHILDREN WITH TIME-OUT IN A CHAIR

This is a good point in the session to introduce the use of time-out in a chair as the primary consequence for noncompliance used in PCIT. Broaching this topic too early in the session is a common mistake, leading parents to think that the therapist is naive to believe that their child will accept time-out without a fight. To avoid parental "yes-butting," the therapist should make sure that the groundwork has been laid and therapist credibility established before tackling this sensitive topic.

The therapist should be prepared for significant resistance when suggesting that time-out can be an effective technique. After all, almost every parent who enters PCIT will have had numerous failure experiences with time-out. A therapeutic strategy that helps decrease resistance is to "read parents' minds." Before parents can list all of the reasons why time-out will not work for their child, the therapist may say something like the following:

> I know what you're probably thinking. You're thinking that I must be crazy if I think Jason is going to go to time-out without a fight. You're also probably thinking that there's no way that Jason will stay in a time-out chair. And, you're thinking that time-out seems like an awfully naive solution to all of Jason's problems. Before you write this off, though, I would like it if you would just hear me out. I've worked with a lot of children with problems just like Jason's, and time-out has been extremely helpful. But, I know that there are at least 100 things that can go wrong with a time-out procedure. Children can lie down flat and refuse to go to the chair. They can hit their parents on the way to time-out. They can knock over the chair, or throw it. If a parent is able to get them to time-out, they can scream obscenities. While in time-out, they can pull their pants down and urinate on the floor. They can take their shoes off and throw them at passersby. They can try to make themselves throw up. Yes, there are many things that have to be worked out. But, if we can get all of the bugs worked out, I believe that time-out is the single most effective consequence for Jason.

Some of the reasons for choosing time-out over other types of consequences can be discussed with the parents: (1) acting-out children are motivated to avoid time-out because it keeps them from stimulating activities, including getting attention from others, (2) nothing is more punishing to young children than complete boredom, (3) unlike some other consequences (e.g., restriction of privileges), time-out can occur within seconds of the inappropriate behavior, (4) unlike spanking, short time-outs can be safely administered numerous times per day, thereby allowing the parent to be more consistent in following through with consequences, (5) time-out does not cause some children to become more aggressive, and (6) time-out is the most commonly used discipline strategy in preschool and elementary school classrooms; use at home will promote greater cross-setting consistency and enhance the child's behavioral adjustment at school as well as at home. Parents may wonder why time-out in a chair is being chosen over time-out in a bedroom or other area.

One reason is that aggressive young children can be destructive when isolated in a room. Another is that they often can find things to entertain themselves with in a bedroom or other area, requiring a lengthier time-out to obtain the same effect.

At this point, the therapist can discuss with the parents how they feel about using time-out. If the parents still are not convinced that the technique has merit, the therapist always can use this strategy:

> I understand your doubts. Jason's behavior can be quite difficult. But, remember that I'm not asking you to go home and try this on your own. Instead, I'll be there coaching you through that first time-out. It will become immediately apparent to both of us whether this approach can help Jason. Given that it has worked with so many other children with problems like his, I have confidence. How about if we just proceed for now with the time-out program? If after next week you still have concerns, we'll reassess. How does that sound?

It is helpful to reassure parents that the child will be taught all of the rules about time-out and minding exercises before any coaching will be conducted.

PRAISING COMPLIANCE

Using the toys, the therapist can role-play possible scenarios for what might happen during the following week's minding exercises. To illustrate, a sample instruction is chosen such as: "Jason, it's almost time for us to leave. Please put Mr. Potato Head back in the box (point to Mr. Potato Head and point to the box)." The therapist can ask the parents to imagine that their child surprised them and quickly put Mr. Potato Head away. How should they respond? By this point in treatment most parents will answer that they should praise their child. What they may not realize is the specificity of the praise that should be provided. Because compliance is the target behavior, the best labeled praises are "Thanks for minding," "I like it when you do what I ask," or "Good following instructions." When enthusiastic labeled praises are given for listening, children begin to view compliance in a more positive light. In addition to the praise for minding, the parent should mention that he or she is happy that the child did not have to go to time-out. Taken together, the best response to a child who complies immediately to a request during minding exercises is something like "Good listening! You did what mommy (daddy) asked you to do and you don't have to go to time-out! I'm very proud of you." Play therapy is then resumed to allow the child to lead for awhile and to decrease any anger the child might have about being required to follow instructions.

THE TWO-CHOICES STATEMENT FOR NONCOMPLIANCE

To explain how the two-choices statement works, the therapist should redirect the parents' attention to the role-play example with Mr. Potato Head. The parents are asked to suppose that the child says, "No, you put Mr. Potato Head away!" Is that a comply or a noncomply? Clearly, the child has not followed the instruction. At this point, the parent must NOT repeat the command. Instead, the parent will simply make a "two-choices statement." The parent holds up two fingers and says in a neutral tone of voice, "You have two choices. You can either put Mr. Potato Head back in the box or go to time-out."

Use of a Visual Signal

Two fingers are used as a visual signal to the inattentive child that this is his or her last chance; the child needs to follow instructions or a consequence will follow. This is described to parents as a kinder and gentler signal than they may have used in the past. Before treatment, most parents repeat instructions to the noncompliant child until they have "had it." The child learns not to comply with instructions the first few times they are issued because he or she knows there is a lot of leeway before the parent will provide a consequence. At the "had it" point, most parents admit that they signal the child with behaviors such as yelling, chasing the child, spanking, and grabbing. This pattern will be replaced by a consistent and predictable sequence of giving a single instruction, counting silently to three seconds to allow the child time to comply, and then using a two-choices statement if the child still has not complied.

The Two-Choices Statement: A Promise, Not a Threat

The two-choices statement must not be taken lightly. The success or failure of the discipline program rests on those two fingers. Whereas parents may occasionally give instructions that they do not follow through on, it is critical that they *never* provide a two-choices statement without being prepared to follow through with time-out. Parents are told to regard the two-choices statement as a serious promise, not an idle threat. The parent is making a promise to the child that a time-out will definitely be forthcoming if the child does not comply. After numerous trials during which the parent follows through with 100% consistency, few children continue to doubt the parent's resolve. Children learn to accept that when a two-choices statement is given, the parent is prepared to follow through with the consequence.

Once the child stops testing the limits, the parents have a powerful discipline tool at their disposal! Rather than having to yell or chase the child to gain compliance, they can provide the kinder and gentler signal of raising two fingers and using a conversational tone of voice. The child will accept that the parent "means what he (or she) says and says what he (or she) means." Within a couple of weeks of beginning the discipline program, most children choose to mind rather than receiving the predictable time-out consequence.

Once the two-choices statement is given, parents are taught to watch closely to determine whether the child has or has not complied. If the child minds, an enthusiastic labeled praise should be given (e.g., "Good listening! I'm glad you followed instructions so you don't have to go to time-out. Now we can play what you want to play"). If the child chooses not to obey, the parent should proceed with time-out.

STRUCTURAL ISSUES ASSOCIATED WITH TIME-OUT

Placement of the Time-out Chair

Most parents believe that time-out needs to be done with the child's nose in a corner or with the child near a wall. One reason to avoid time-out in a corner is its long history of use as punishment through "humiliation." However, there are other reasons to avoid this practice. It is helpful for the therapist to put a chair in a corner and role-play for the parent what likely will happen. When an active, defiant child is placed within kicking distance of a wall, it is a safe bet that his or her feet will end up on the wall. If the child is placed within reach of magazines, cupboards, wallpaper, etc., it is very likely that the child's hands will be on everything within grasp. To avoid these common problems, parents should place the time-out chair so that it is in the "middle of nothing." A good strategy is to sit in the time-out chair and reach out in all directions. If nothing can be touched within that radius, the location will do well for time-out. Effort should also be made to minimize extraneous entertainment during time-out. The child should not be in view of the television and should not be placed in a high-traffic area where siblings will be unduly tempted to interact with the child in time-out.

Choosing the Time-out Chair

A common pitfall of time-out is choosing an inappropriate time-out chair. Children's anger can reach high levels during time-out, and the chair needs to be sturdy enough to withstand destructive behavior. One misconception is that children should have time-out in a child-sized chair. An adult-sized chair is much more effective for several reasons: it is more difficult to fall out of, it is less likely to tip over, and it discourages impulsive young children from hopping out because their feet do not touch the floor. Some children will bite, scratch, and poke holes in the time-out chair, so expensive chairs should be avoided. Heavily cushioned chairs, rocking chairs, and chairs that have rollers are less effective because they can be fun and relaxing. The best all-around choice for a time-out chair is a solid, wooden kitchen chair with no arms, which can be pulled into the middle of a room as needed. For coaching time-out in the clinic, it is best to avoid light plastic chairs because they tip over easily and children tend to slide off of them. A wooden or heavy metal chair with a fabric or vinyl-covered seat is a good choice.

GETTING THE CHILD TO TIME-OUT

Reviewing the Sequence

To help parents follow the sequence of events, the therapist can repeat earlier lessons by returning to the original role-play. Instruction is as follows: "Jason, it's almost time to go (reason given before command). Please put Mr. Potato Head back in the box (direct command)." Jason responds, "No. You put Mr. Potato Head away!" The parent is then asked what happens next in the sequence. The correct answer is that the parent says, "You have two choices. You can either put Mr. Potato Head away or go to time-out." Suppose Jason says, "No! I'm busy!" The parent is asked whether this is a comply or noncomply. Because it is a noncomply, the child must be sent to time-out as promised.

What Problem Behaviors Will Occur on the Way to Time-out?

Parents are asked what will happen when they try to get "Jason" from his seat at the table to the time-out chair across the room. To interject some humor, parents can be asked, "Will Jason walk over there like a little gentleman when you ask him to?" Parents usually respond with a series of anticipated problems (e.g., child grabs hold of their seat, dives under the table, runs out the door, goes limp, lies flat on the floor, hits the parent). Parents often overestimate the amount of resistance their children will show. We do not consider this to be a problem because it enables us to problem-solve concerning worst-case scenarios. The fact that we take this information in stride reinforces our credibility with parents. We find that role-playing is the best method for teaching parents how to get their children to time-out.

Escorting a Cooperative Child to Time-out

The therapist should display the best way to escort a cooperative child to time-out. If "Jason" is willing to be escorted, the parent should stand up, gently take him by the hand, and walk him to time-out while saying the following: "You didn't choose to mind. So you have to sit on the chair." Once Jason is placed on the chair, the parent says, "Stay on the chair until I tell you you can get off." The parent then walks away quickly. It is explained that children are less likely to resist going to time-out if the parent moves quickly and confidently. They are instructed to limit their speech to the two sentences noted above and to use all of their control to maintain a neutral facial expression and voice tone.

Using the "Barrel Carry" with Resistive Children

After having completed the behavioral play therapy portion of PCIT, most young children surprise their parents with how cooperative they are when instructed to go to time-out. However, realizing that some highly aggressive children are uncooperative regarding time-out, the therapist should next display the technique for getting a defiant young child to time-out. When the child will not walk to time-out on his or her own, the parent must carry the child. The safest carry is the "barrel carry," where the parent wraps his or her arms around the child (under the child's arms and across the chest) as if holding onto a barrel. Given that a face-to-face carry would be potentially dangerous to the parent and the child (e.g., the child can hit and kick harder from that position and can butt his or her own head into the parent's), the child's back should be against the parent's chest. To secure the carry, the parent can hold onto his or her own right wrist with the other hand. Parents are instructed that dragging children by the arms or legs is dangerous and should never be done.

Managing Aggressive Behavior on the Way to Time-out

In the barrel carry, the child's arms and legs remain free. For that reason, children are capable of hitting, kicking, pinching, and hair pulling on the way to the time-out chair. To reduce the likelihood of the child physically attacking the parent, the time-out chair is positioned nearby. Also, the parent is instructed to move quickly and confidently when taking the child to time-out. However, the possibility always exists that the child could strike the parent on the way to time-out.

Employing a doll, role-playing can be used to demonstrate how the child could hit or kick from the barrel hold. Parents are asked about the possible ways they could respond to this behavior. It is then illustrated to the parent that any response in this situation will only serve to escalate the child's aggression. For example, if the parent says, "Don't you hit me!," the child will be reinforced by the fact that the angry attempt to get negative attention was successful. Thus, the parent is instructed to ignore all strikes and to continue moving the child to time-out as quickly as possible. If hitting is completely ignored, it rarely continues past the first one or two time-out episodes. If it is not eliminated through ignoring, strategies (e.g., adding extra time in time-out, developing a behavior contract) can be used later in the program to decrease aggression.

WHAT IF THE CHILD AGREES TO COMPLY ON THE WAY TO TIME-OUT?

A common "tough call" occurs when the child begins complying after the time-out process has been initiated. For example, the parent has given the child the two-choices statement, but the child has ignored the parent. Then, the parent stands up, takes the child by the hand, and begins to escort the child to time-out. Once the oppositional child realizes that the parent intends to follow through on the consequence, Mr. Potato Head is desperately thrown into the box in a last-second attempt to avoid time-out!

While this may seem like a minor technicality, it actually can be a critical point in the discipline program. When children learn that they can wait until their parent stands up before compliance is required, they seldom will follow instructions when their parent is seated or at a distance. This problem can be avoided if the parent takes the child to time-out the first several times this limit testing occurs. Thus, the parent would stand up and take the child by the hand. The child would try to comply even though the time has expired. The parent continues to take the child to time-out while using a slight modification of the original words: "You didn't choose to mind quickly enough, so you have to go to time-out. Stay on the chair until I tell you you can get off."

WHAT IF THE CHILD TAKES A TOY TO TIME-OUT?

Occasionally, children will try to take toys or objects with them to time-out. Because time-out is a restriction of the privilege to have stimulation and attention, it is important that children not be permitted to play during this time. The best parental response is to quickly take the toy from the child's hand. The parent should avoid saying anything such as "Give me that toy." The child is highly unlikely to follow this instruction, and will be rewarded by the negative attention.

LENGTH OF TIME-OUT

Why Three Minutes?

Once the child is placed in time-out, the parent should start timing. The typical time-out period in PCIT is three minutes. With clinic-referred children, we do not use the often-repeated rule of thumb, "one minute for each year of age." We agree that this is a good guideline for children who do not have severe behavior problems. However, for an extremely active and disorganized five-year-old, five minutes would likely be too long, and thereby set the child up to fail. Instead, three minutes was chosen because it is the shortest time-out period that is effective.

The "Five Seconds of Silence" Rule

Extra time may be added to the three-minute time-out because of disruptive behavior in the chair. Before the parent asks the child if he or she is ready to mind, the child must be silent for five seconds. The purpose of the latter condition is to prevent superstitious learning. Suppose the child had just yelled at the parent, "I hate you! You're so mean!," and because the three minutes happened to be up the parent walked over to ask if the child was ready to mind. The child could superstitiously learn that hateful remarks are the way to controlling time-out. Instead, once the time reaches 2 minutes and 55 seconds, the parent should begin to slowly and silently count to five. If the child talks, cries, screams, or pounds on the chair during that period, the parent will begin the silent count to five again. The three minutes does *not* begin again just because the child is disruptive. Only the five-second count starts over. Once the child is quiet for five seconds, the parent should hurry over to the chair, stand out of the reach of the child, and say, "Now that you are quiet, are you ready to come back and put Mr. Potato Head in the box now?" The "now that you are quiet" phrase teaches the child that it is the quiet that encourages the parent to end time-out, not the crying or yelling.

Shaping Children to Sit for the Full Three Minutes

The "typical" time-out period is three minutes. However, for some children, the therapist may choose to require less than three minutes initially, with the intention of shaping the child's sitting to an ultimate three-minute goal. Examples of children for whom we have used shaping include the following: (1) an extremely disorganized eight-year-old girl who was diagnosed with fetal alcohol syndrome and had an estimated attention span of 30 seconds, (2) a 23-month-old who was displaying more than 20 temper tantrums a day, (3) an aggressive four-year-old whose skilled foster parent indicated that she had never been able to keep him in time-out for longer than 20 seconds, (4) a three-and-a-half-year-old boy diagnosed with an attention deficit hyperactivity disorder who had been expelled from eight day-care centers, and (5) a four-year-old diagnosed with pervasive developmental disorder.

In each of these cases, we felt that the child was not initially capable of sitting in time-out for the full three minutes. Thus, a time-out period was established for each child that we felt would be achievable (usually between 20 and 45 seconds). When the allotted seconds had passed, parents were told to hurry over and reinforce the sitting by saying, "Since you're sitting in time-out so well, are you ready to come back and put Mr. Potato Head in the box?" Arguably, there is little to be lost by attempting this shaping procedure. If the child chooses to mind, the shorter time-out is a clear success. If the child chooses not to mind, the time-out simply can be repeated using a greater time interval. An overall benefit of shaping rather than requiring a full three-minute time-out immediately is that it increases the likelihood of a mastery experience during the child's first clinic time-out. That mastery experience can then be reinforced and built on during subsequent time-outs. A disadvantage of shaping is that the parent receives less coaching in how to handle time-out escape because the child does not get out of time-out as often. The parents, therefore, may find themselves ill-prepared to handle time-out escapes during practice sessions at home.

COMMON MISBEHAVIORS IN THE TIME-OUT CHAIR

Returning to role-playing, suppose that the child refused to put Mr. Potato Head away when given the two-choices statement and has been taken to time-out. The parents should now be asked about behaviors that their child is likely to exhibit while in time-out. Inevitably, parents point out that their child will not stay in time-out, and they try to get the therapist to explain immediately what to do when the child escapes. We typically tell parents that they have asked a very important question because few of the children seen in PCIT will stay in time-out without a foolproof plan. The parent is reassured that they will not leave the session without knowing that plan, but it takes a long time to explain and it will make more sense to talk about it later in the session. For now, the parents are asked to pretend that their child has been "superglued" to the chair and cannot escape, and they are invited to list all of the behaviors the child might display.

Ignoring All Verbalizations

Parents typically anticipate that their child will cry, scream, talk, whine, call them names, and ask questions like "Can I get up now?" The parent is instructed to ignore *all* verbalizations. Role-playing is often helpful to demonstrate proper ignoring. No direct eye contact should be made with the child, though the parent is expected to surreptitiously watch the child. The parent should not show disgust, amusement, or irritation. Instead, the parent's face should be as neutral and expressionless as a robot's.

"I Have to Go to the Bathroom"

One situation that we always try to discuss with parents ahead of time is how to handle when the child says he or she has to go to the bathroom. This is a common ploy to avoid time-out. It is explained to parents that most children can "hold it" for three minutes and that their pleas to go to the bathroom are usually an attempt to get out of time-out. Parents are asked what would happen in future time-outs if they allow their child to go to the bathroom during the first time-out experiences. Recognizing the precedent that can be set, most parents indicate that they feel comfortable ignoring the request. However, some children participating in PCIT are either going through toilet training or have just mastered this developmental milestone. Their parents may not be comfortable denying their requests to go to the bathroom. To prevent this problem, we encourage parents to take their children to the bathroom before the beginning of clinic sessions and home practice sessions. If a child undergoing toilet training requests a bathroom break and the parent is not comfortable ignoring the request, the parent may choose to quickly take the child to the toilet and then return the child immediately to time-out. Parents are instructed that if bathroom requests become habitual during time-out, it is a clear indicator that they are a delay tactic that should be ignored.

Time-out Does Not End until the Original Instruction Is Obeyed

Following through with the original instruction after the time-out is critical to the success of this program and is a common flaw in the disciplinary approaches being used in many day cares and homes. Learning to mind does not occur during time-out or because of time-out. It occurs when the child has an opportunity to "replay" the original situation with a different ending. Rather than receiving a negative consequence the second time, the child is able to experience the rewards associated with being cooperative (i.e., parental praise, continuing to play). The message to the child is simple: "You can either mind your parents, or you can go to time-out and then mind your parents. In any case, this will not end until you show that you can listen."

Returning to role-playing, assume that the child is indeed "superglued" to the time-out chair. The parent has ignored all verbalizations from the child during the time-out. At 2 minutes and 55 seconds, the parent begins to count silently to determine when the child achieves five seconds of silence. Once the child has been silent for five seconds, the parent hurries over to the time-out chair. Standing at arm's distance from the child to avoid being grabbed, the parent holds out his or her hand and says, "Since you're sitting quietly, are you ready to come back and put Mr. Potato Head in the box?" The therapist should role-play with the parents all of the possible responses to this question, as a quick judgment must be made regarding whether the child is ready to mind.

Child Refuses to Comply with the Original Directive

One possible situation is for the child to completely ignore the parent when the "Are you ready to ..." question is asked. The parent should count silently to three. If the child has not made an effort to take the parent's hand, the child is considered to be "not ready" to follow instructions. Also, if the child shouts out a defiant "No!" and refuses to take the parent's hand, he or she is not ready to get out of time-out.

For situations in which the child refuses to follow the initial instruction, the parent should say in a neutral tone of voice, "OK, then stay on the chair until I tell you to get off," and walk away. For children who then jump up and try to mind after the fact, parents should return them to time-out and say, "You didn't choose to mind quickly enough, so you have to go back to time-out. Stay on the chair until I tell you to get off."

In rare cases, children will repeatedly refuse to obey the original instruction, even after as many as seven time-outs. To avoid leaving children in time-out for excessive periods, we use a guideline of 20 consecutive minutes as the longest interval that a child may remain in time-out. If the child has not agreed to comply by that point, the parent is advised to use a "physical prompt." The time-out is ended by having the parent physically guide the child's hand to comply with at least a portion of the original instruction (e.g., parent guides child's hand to pick up Mr. Potato Head's eyes and place them in the box).

Child Agrees to Comply with the Original Directive

If a child makes any attempt to return to the table when asked about readiness to mind, the child is considered ready to comply. This is the case even when a child does so with a negative attitude. Once back at the table, the parent may point to clarify the instruction. However, the original instruction should not be made again because it was repeated when the child was asked if he or she was ready to comply. Sometimes a child will refuse, argue, or ignore the parent at this point. The parent then should provide the two-choices statement: "You have two choices. You can either put Mr. Potato Head back in the box or go back to time-out." If the child does not comply, the time-out sequence is repeated.

Use of a Second Instruction to Overteach Compliance

Suppose the child returns to the table and complies with the original command. Contrary to what the parent might expect, it is best for the parent to avoid praising the child at this point. After all, a time-out was required to obtain compliance with the simple instruction. Instead, the parent can simply acknowledge that the child complied using words such as "all right," "thank you," or "OK." Immediately thereafter, the child is given a second command that is very similar to the one that resulted in time-out (e.g., "Now, please put the car back in the box"). When the child complies with the second instruction (which nearly all children do right after having had a time-out), enthusiastic labeled praises should be provided. Here's an example: "Thanks for following instructions so well! I'm proud of you for learning to listen. When you choose to mind, you don't have to go to time-out. Now we can play what you want to play."

The enthusiastic praise should sharply contrast with the acknowledgment given for the child's first compliance. Through this process of making the contingencies for compliance and noncompliance crystal clear, the child learns to view compliance in a more positive light. After all, compliance leads to enthusiastic praise and a continuance of play. Noncompliance leads to a time-out, eventual compliance, and an unenthusiastic acknowledgment. With practice, compliance begins to replace noncompliance as the more rewarding behavior and oppositionality diminishes.

USE OF PLAY THERAPY TO DECREASE THE CHILD'S ANGER LEVEL

Oppositional children become angry when learning to follow instructions. In the beginning it is difficult for them to lose some of the control that they have had over their parents. Behavioral play therapy skills serve an important role not only in bringing that anger level down, but also in helping children view compliance in a more positive light. A major goal of PCIT is to develop some give-and-take in the parent–child relationship. During play therapy, the parent allows the child to lead the play and is respectful of the child's desires. When an instruction is given, it is the parent's time to lead the play and the child learns to reciprocate by showing respect for the parent's desires. Through this process, the child comes to view minding as a routine courtesy that leads to family harmony, parental approval, and positive attention. This allows the child to develop skills as both a leader and a follower and forms the basis of the early social skill of turn-taking. Therefore, during clinic coaching, a few minutes of play therapy follow each instance of compliance. As much as ten minutes may be needed following a time-out sequence to reduce the child's anger and deal with any distance that might have occurred in the parent–child relationship.

FOUR TIME-OUT BEHAVIORS THAT CANNOT BE IGNORED

Time-out Escape

If an oppositional child realizes that the parent is unable to enforce time-out, time-out will not work. A common time-out escape is the child jumping out of the chair immediately after being placed there. Other children are able to sit for a minute or so and then become so agitated that they impulsively get out of time-out (shaping the sitting behavior would be appropriate for this child). Sometimes there are tough calls regarding whether a child has escaped or not. For example, many children become gymnasts in time-out, spinning and lying across the chair. During the course of this activity, they often "accidentally" fall off and look up to the parent to determine how this will be handled. It is important for this behavior to *not* be ignored as the child will test the limits further if the original test is successful. Similarly, children can be observed to progressively slide their bodies farther and farther out of the chair until only their shoulder blades are on the chair or in some cases they have only a hand remaining in time-out. For these tough calls, parents are given a "50% of the body weight" rule. Once 51% of the child's body weight is off of the chair, the child is considered to have gotten out of time-out.

Scooting or Vigorous Rocking of the Time-out Chair

Although scooting or rocking the chair can initially seem rather innocuous, it quickly becomes a major problem when ignored. The child can scoot the chair over to toys, to the mother's purse, to breakable artwork, and so forth. Scooting or rocking is stimulating enough that it can be a source of reinforcement to the child. As such, children need to be informed that scooting and rocking the time-out chair are not permissible and will lead to a negative consequence.

Standing on the Time-out Chair

This problem is most frequent with two- and three-year-olds. When placed in time-out, these children often turn around on their knees and hold onto the back of the chair in order to look at the parent (an acceptable behavior). After being ignored, they may actually stand on the chair. This is a dangerous behavior regardless of the age of the child. To protect the child, potentially dangerous behavior must be handled assertively, using backup contingencies to be discussed later.

Self-Injurious Behavior

On occasion, acting-out young children may engage in minor self-injurious behavior while in time-out. For example, a child might repeatedly hit his head on the padded part of the chair in such a way as to obtain stimulation without causing a bruise or scratch. Similarly, a child might bite down on the back of her hand to release frustration, but being careful not to actually draw blood. Slapping the face lightly and pulling hair also might be observed. Any self-injurious behavior that causes harm to the child in the form of scratches, drawing blood, or leaving a bruise cannot be ignored. The two populations most likely to demonstrate this type of dangerous self-injurious behavior are children with developmental disabilities and children who have been abused or neglected. In summary, whereas minor self-stimulating behaviors can be ignored, behaviors that are causing harm to the child must be stopped.

BACKUPS FOR TIME-OUT ESCAPE AND OTHER BEHAVIORS THAT CANNOT BE IGNORED

There are several consequences that can be used when children engage in one of the time-out behaviors that cannot be ignored. The therapist must use sound clinical judgment when choosing the best backup for a particular family, and the choice of procedure should always include parental input. Factors to be considered include the following: (1) therapist comfort with the procedure, (2) parent comfort with the procedure, (3) child's developmental level, (4) parental skill level and history of use of physical discipline, and (5) severity of the child's behavior problems. There is no perfect backup to time-out, and all of the options we present have strengths and weaknesses. In any case, teaching a defiant young child to stay in time-out is extremely difficult. Therapists should realize that the most effective strategies for preventing time-out escape also are the most confrontive and controversial. We do not expressly endorse any of the procedures described here, but present them as options for clinicians and families to consider.

Two Swats on the Bottom

A two-swat spank on the buttocks with the hand has traditionally been used in Hanf–Model programs as a consequence for time-out escape (e.g., Forehand & McMahon, 1981). The first time the child exits time-out, a warning is given: "You got off of the chair before I told you you could. If you get off of the chair again before I tell you to, I will spank you." From then on, every time the child leaves time-out without permission, the parent sits down on the time-out chair, bends the child over one knee, pulls the child's pants down, and delivers two swats on the bare buttocks. The purpose of swatting on the bare buttocks is to deliver swats that the child can feel without undue force being used, *not* to humiliate the child. Spanking through clothing is not as safe because it requires more parental force to be effective, and parents have a harder time judging the strength of the swats.

An advantage of this technique is that children rapidly learn to stay in the chair. This happens largely because the consequence is truly aversive and occurs within seconds of the undesirable behavior (no lengthy delay as in restriction of privileges). *It is uncommon for children to need more than two spanks to learn to accept time-out.* Proponents of this procedure argue that the majority of U.S. parents of young children already use spanking. Spanking is a legal and socially tolerated method of disciplining young children, and most parents of children with behavior disorders are spanking several times each day. If time-out fails, in all likelihood these parents will return to daily spanking. However, if an effective technique can be used to teach the child to stay in the chair, time-out will become a very powerful tool for improving the child's behavior and spanking can then be eliminated from the parent's discipline repertoire. So, by sanctioning the use of approximately two spanks over the course of treatment, there is a good chance of eliminating spanking entirely.

The disadvantages of this approach are largely related to the controversy over whether spanking is an appropriate form of discipline and whether it should be endorsed in any form by professionals who advocate for children. Spanking has been banned in most school districts and day-care centers across the country because of the belief that it is harmful to children. Many mental health professionals have a moral opposition to spanking. This stems in part from observations that spanking is associated with high levels of aggression in children (although a causal link has not been established), as well as the belief that the technique is disrespectful of the child as an individual. Understandably, many professionals will have a difficult time incorporating this technique into PCIT. Furthermore, parents with histories of child maltreatment may not able to spank in a controlled fashion. Those involved with the child welfare system, for example, are often restricted from spanking at the risk of forfeiting custody of their child. We specifically caution that children with histories of physical abuse not receive swats as the backup to time-out. When all of the pros and cons are considered together, it is clear that very careful judgments must be made as to whether spanking as a backup is appropriate for individual therapists, children, and parents.

The Two-Chair Hold Procedure

Because there are many situations in which spanking cannot be used as the backup, we have experimented with a variety of alternative procedures. One that we have had some initial success with is the two-chair hold procedure.* The basis of the two-chair technique is as follows: If a child escapes from the time-out chair after an initial warning, he or she will be taken by the parent to a second chair ("the hold chair") for a brief movement restriction consequence (McNeil, Clemens-Mowrer, Gurwitch, & Funderburk, 1994). The hold used is the "single basket control technique" (e.g., Wyka & Gabriel, 1987) modified for a sitting position. Seated in a chair behind the hold chair, the parent crosses the child's arms such that the child's lower arm is locked under the upper elbow. Following a hold of approximately 45 seconds, the child is placed back in the time-out chair. He or she is then given an opportunity to comply with the original command after sitting independently in the regular time-out chair for only five seconds. Sitting behavior in the time-out chair is shaped to increasing approximations of an ultimate three-minute goal. Particularly with very impulsive two-year-olds, we have had some success using washable hand-stamps as a quickly administered reinforcer for good sitting during the shaping process.

If the child refuses to sit independently in time-out for five seconds after the first hold, a second hold is conducted for 90 seconds. Then the child is placed back in the time-out chair in another attempt to achieve five seconds of independent sitting. For any child escaping a third time, a three-minute hold is used, followed by a final attempt to obtain five seconds of independent sitting. In the interest of safety, the procedure is ended after the third hold through the use of a physical prompt (i.e., the parent physically guides the child's hand to comply with the original request) and play therapy is continued.

In the development of the two-chair procedure, much attention was paid to developing a hold that provided minimal reinforcement to the child. That is why

*The remainder of this paragraph, and the next three paragraphs, is adapted from McNeil, Clemens-Mowrer, Gurwitch, and Funderburk, 1994, with permission.

parents hold the child from behind the chair rather than holding the child on their lap. During the hold, the parent is instructed to avoid eye contact with the child and to remain silent. Additionally, in contrast to other hold techniques (e.g., Barkley, 1987), the regular time-out chair is separate from the "hold" chair. It was hypothesized that being held in a second chair would be less reinforcing than being held in the regular time-out chair. The reinforcing value of a one-chair system is obvious: the young child can sit alone on the chair, or he or she can escape and receive some comfort and attention by being held. In the two-chair hold procedure, it becomes clear to the young child both that he or she can choose to be held, but that time-out will not end until the child sits independently in the regular time-out chair. For children who find the hold rewarding or "funny," a restriction of privilege can be paired with the hold to create a more negative consequence.

Unlike some previously described immobilization techniques (e.g., Luiselli, Suskin, & Slocumb, 1984), the determining factor for release from the safe hold is time, not calm and quiet behavior from the child. This decision was made because pilot trials showed that defiant children often take 20 minutes or longer to calm down and that parents had a difficult time maintaining an extended hold that was safe and effective.

An advantage of the two-chair hold procedure is that most children learn to stay in time-out after fewer than three brief holds (McNeil *et al.*, 1994). Disadvantages include the fact that the hold technique is a confrontive, physical technique that may be interpreted as disrespectful to children. Another limitation is that the shaping procedure is quite complicated and difficult to teach to parents. Some intellectually limited parents may never learn to provide the procedure safely and effectively. Furthermore, special training in the use of restraints is advisable for therapists to gain competency in the use of this physical approach. The two-chair technique is not recommended for children ages six and older because it is difficult for parents to safely restrain children of that size. Finally, the technique also may not be appropriate for some abusive parents who are unable to safely implement any type of physical discipline method.

Isolation in Another Room

One option for children who refuse to stay in a time-out chair is to send them to another room (usually a bedroom) as a backup (Webster-Stratton, 1993). For coaching purposes, the analogous backup is the use of a room without toys or furniture. In this procedure, the child is sent to a time-out chair. If the child refuses to stay in the chair, the parent warns the child that he or she will be sent to the room the next time the child gets off the chair. Then, if the child gets up a second time, the child is taken to the room. If necessary, the parent may hold onto the doorknob to prevent time-out escape.

An advantage of this approach is that it involves less physical confrontation between the parent and child. For parents with anger control difficulties, this may be a better choice than either the hold or the spank. Also, older children who are too large to be spanked or held may do better with this less physical approach. A disadvantage of this procedure is that the parent cannot visually monitor the child during the time-out [see Day and Roberts (1983) for a variation called the Barrier Method which involves having visual contact but is impractical for use in many homes]. Children who are aggressive and destructive can do extensive damage to the room and possibly hurt themselves in the process. Another disadvantage is that some children, usually those who have stimulating activities in their room, are not optimally motivated by this consequence. Finally, the process of having the parent hold the doorknob can become a challenge to an aggressive child. Sometimes children's aggression can escalate as the back-and-forth pulling at the door continues. Parents may inquire about the appropriateness of putting a lock on the outside of the door. Problems with a lock include the possibility that the parent will abuse the process by leaving the child isolated for excessive periods of time and concerns about fire safety.

Restriction of Privileges

For most acting-out preschoolers, restriction of privileges is a consequence that is too delayed to have an immediate effect on time-out escape. However, it can be used effectively with some six- to eight-year-olds. The parent and child make a list of privileges that can be restricted. Emphasis is placed on using the smallest privilege possible to obtain the desired behavior (e.g., instead of taking away a bike for a week, restrict it for one afternoon). The first time the child refuses to stay in time-out, a warning is given about the specific privilege that will be lost should the child get up a second time. When the child gets up again, the parent says, "You chose not to stay in time-out, so you won't be able to watch *The Simpsons* tonight." At that point, the time-out is ended.

One disadvantage of this approach is that the child may not comply with the original directive. For example, suppose that "Doug" is told to put on his coat but refuses. His parent tells him that he has two choices: he can put on his coat or go to time-out. Doug fails to respond to the two-choices statement and his parent takes him to time-out. Instead of sitting appropriately, Doug escapes and his parent must take him back to time-out. Doug's parent tells him that if he runs away again he will not get to play Nintendo for two nights. When Doug escapes from time-out a second time, his parent says, "No Nintendo." At this point, the parent has played his or her last card and Doug still does not have his coat on. If this occurs during the first five minutes of the session, the therapist also has used up his or her last card and cannot easily regain cooperation from Doug to continue the session.

An advantage of this approach is that it can be conducted without any physical intervention. For some parents, hands-on techniques are not safe. Other parents do not have the physical strength to perform any of the physical backups successfully. Another advantage is that it can be combined with other approaches to make them more effective as in the following examples: (1) "If I have to hold you in the holding chair, you will not be able to play with your Legos today" or (2) "You have two choices. You can either stay in your room, or you will have to miss out on swimming tomorrow. You choose."

Handling Time-Out Escape in Children with Minor Behavior Problems

For children with less severe behavior problems, there are a number of methods that can be successfully employed to teach them to stay in time-out. However, each has major flaws when used with severely disruptive children. Alternatives for subclinical populations include: (1) standing by the time-out chair, (2) placing a hand on the child's shoulder as he or she sits in time-out, (3) repeatedly placing the child back in the timeout chair, (4) adding additional time for time-out escapes, and (5) explaining to the child that time-out does not begin until he or she sits appropriately.

ROLE-PLAYING AND WRAP-UP

Once the therapist and parents have agreed on the best backup for time-out escape, the entire time-out procedure is reviewed using role-playing. Incorporating humor, the parents can role-play taking the therapist to time-out. If using either a hold or spank, it is critical that the parent practice these skills before using them. For the hold procedure, practice can be conducted using a doll, a spouse, or the therapist as a child substitute. The parents must demonstrate the proper crossing of the child's arms for this technique. For the spank, the therapist spanks his or her own arm with the fingertips, demonstrating the proper strength to be used. Then each parent is asked to swat their own arm to experience the feeling and receive feedback from the therapist regarding the amount of force used. Suggested role-plays include:

1	Giving a well-stated, direct command (reason first).
2	Child complies (follow with labeled praise).
3	Child fails to comply (follow with two-choices statement).
4	Child defies two-choices statement (escort child to time-out).
5	Child screams in time-out (ignore all verbalizations).
6	Child stays full three minutes and achieves five seconds of silence (ask if child is ready to comply).
7	Child refuses to comply when asked if ready (repeat time-out).
8	Child agrees to comply when asked if ready (escort child back to table and gesture to indicate instruction).
9	Child complies with original instruction (acknowledge and provide second, very similar instruction).

10	Child complies with second instruction (provide enthusiastic labeled praise, tell child that time-out was avoided by agreeing to comply, return to play therapy to decrease anger).
11	Child refuses to sit in time-out (provide warning the first time; if it happens a second time, follow through with the predetermined consequence).

Prior to the next session, parents should review the discipline diagram (see Appendix) and attempt to memorize the dialogue. The importance of NOT using the time-out skills before the next session is stressed. The first time-out sets a precedent for all that follows. If the parents attempt it at home and something goes wrong, it will be very difficult to backtrack and reteach the child. If, however, the first time-out occurs in the clinic, the parents will have the therapist to coach them through it. This will ensure that the first time-out is successful, thereby setting the stage for successful time-outs in the future. The parents are asked to promise the therapist that they will not try any of the time-out techniques taught in this session until they have had a chance to be coached first.

The homework assignment for the upcoming week is: (1) practice rephrasing commands as described early in the session, (2) provide specific labeled praises for following instructions, and (3) continue five minutes of daily behavioral play therapy. Parents leave the session with a play therapy homework sheet and discipline handouts (rules for giving good directions and discipline diagram).

The First Discipline Coaching Session

Novice therapists should memorize the discipline diagram (see Appendix) before entering the session. Because coaching decisions must be made quickly, complete knowledge of the standardized dialogue and sequence of the discipline program is critical. In the beginning, it is helpful for therapists to prepare a "cheat sheet" of good instructions and coaching examples. In addition, the following items are needed for the session: (1) stickers or treats for behavioral rehearsals, (2) a play therapy homework sheet, and (3) a discipline homework sheet (see Appendix).

Two hours should be set aside for the first discipline coaching session. While 75 minutes may be adequate, there must be sufficient time for handling time-outs that occur toward the end of the session. The session cannot end until the child has complied and the parent and child have had an opportunity to work through any upsetting feelings using play therapy. In two-parent families, each parent is coached separately with the child for approximately half of the session.

The playroom furniture should consist of a table, two chairs at the table for the interaction, and the sturdy time-out chair(s). If the two-chair hold technique is being used, two time-out chairs are positioned out of reach of the table and each other. A smaller chair is placed behind the hold chair so that the parent can sit comfortably during the procedure. Once the therapist leaves the room, the parent is told to slide the table in front of the door to discourage the child from running out of the room, but not blocking it in case safety issues arise.

Toys are chosen carefully. To enhance coaching, the toy selection should include ones that are both desirable and undesirable to the particular child. The "less desirable" activities can be used to teach children to comply with more challenging instructions. We avoid heavy toys that can break the observation mirror or become dangerous projectiles when thrown.

Throughout the discipline program portion of this book, we make the assumption that therapists will conduct their coaching from an observation room via the bug-in-ear device. We prefer this method over in-room coaching during the initial steps of the discipline program. Early on, we are highly directive in our coaching and we find that the flow of parent–child communication is less disrupted when we make our remarks privately to the parent over the bug-in-ear. We also believe it is important for children to perceive that it is the parent who is giving directives and "in charge." When the child hears the therapist telling the parents which words to use, the parent's authority may be compromised in the eyes of the child. However, we recognize that not all PCIT therapists will have access to bug-in-ear technology and we do not consider it to be critical. We have been successful in coaching all of the discipline program procedures from within the playroom.

BEGINNING THE SESSION

The child plays at the table while the therapist and parent(s) review the week and the discipline procedure. Parents are asked about their play therapy homework. We encourage them to place an even higher priority on the play therapy practice as the discipline program gets under way. The therapist reiterates that play therapy is important for offsetting the anger and attitude problems that may arise when limits are suddenly enforced. The parents are then asked whether they had an opportunity to study the discipline diagram. A review of the diagram takes place by briefly rehearsing the entire command and time-out sequence.

At the end of the review, we routinely ask parents whether they are physically and emotionally ready to "go the distance" with the time-out procedure. The therapist should not accept "I think so" as an answer. When parents exhibit any hesitation, they are told that a 100% commitment is needed before proceeding. We explain that the worst scenario during the first discipline coaching session would be for them to "give up" in the middle of a stressful time-out. The child would receive the message that "if I just cry, fight, scream, and run away, my mom (or dad) will let me have my way." So, to begin the first discipline coaching session, a firm commitment is needed from the parents ensuring that they are willing to follow the discipline sequence through to completion. If a parent appears depressed, tired, irritable, or hesitant, the therapist should encourage the family to delay the beginning of the discipline program and coach play therapy instead.

REHEARSING TIME-OUT WITH THE CHILD: "TELL–SHOW–DO–REVIEW"

Fairness dictates that children be informed of new rules and consequences before they are implemented. Whereas parents commonly wait until the "heat of the battle" to explain the upcoming consequences, we believe that children are most receptive to learning new rules when they are calm and cooperative. We have experimented with various ways of educating young children in advance about the expectations for minding exercises and the time-out procedure. Even very young children have cognitive resources that can be tapped to help the discipline program be implemented more smoothly. They adapt to the new discipline program more readily when the therapist is proactive in using the following simple teaching sequence: "tell–show–do–review."

There are a number of time-out skills that children with behavioral disorders must learn. They need to learn to walk to time-out by themselves, to sit in time-out without major disruptions, and to stay in time-out for the allotted time. If time-out behavior is viewed in the same light as behaviors such as writing one's name or riding a bike, it makes sense to use a "tell–show–do–review" approach. In other words, children can learn this skill through explanation, modeling of appropriate behavior, practice, rewards for successive approximations, and repetition. Positive practice in a "pretend" situation can enhance the child's ability to have successful time-outs during the coaching and at home.

We always have the parents review the discipline program with the children before the coaching session begins. This is done by carefully coaching the parents through the explanation, modeling, and rehearsal. Because most preschoolers have very short attention spans, the process must move quickly (i.e., take no more than three to five minutes). We usually ask parents to repeat our exact words. To enlist the child's cooperation, small tangible rewards are used. The steps are as follows:

1	Move the child's chair away from the toys to encourage greater attention.
2	Show the child the stickers or treats and indicate that they can earn these prizes by listening carefully to some instructions.
3	Explain minding exercises in a way that the child can understand. For example: "Today our playtime is going to be a little different. Today we are going to practice minding. I'm going to tell you lots of little things to do . . . like hand me the man, put the eyes on Mr. Potato Head, or put one block on top of another block. But, this is not a game. It is very important that you learn to listen. If you mind, I'll be very proud of you and we can keep playing. If you don't mind, you'll have to go to time-out like this" (parent walks over to the time-out chair and sits down).
4	Explain time-out length and silence requirement. As parent is sitting in time-out, an explanation such as the following is given to the child: "When you are in time-out, you have to be quiet, like a mouse. If you cry or yell or say, 'Mommy, can I get up?,' I won't look at you or talk to you. The rule of time-out is that I can't talk to you at all when you are in time-out. You have to stay in time-out for three minutes. Then, when I can see that you're being quiet like a mouse, I will come over to time-out and see if you are ready to follow instructions."

5 Explain backup for time-out escape. While still sitting in the time-out chair, the parent should mimic getting out of time-out and say, "You are not allowed to get out of time-out until I tell you to." If the parent feels the child is likely to engage in one of the other problematic behaviors (e.g., scooting, rocking, self-injury, standing in the chair), that rule can be discussed as well: "And, you are not allowed to scoot the chair like this." Then, the parent should explain the predetermined backup plan. Here is an example of how the two-chair hold would be explained to the child: "If you get out of time-out, even a little bit like this, you will have to go to this holding chair. I will cross your arms like this (parent crosses own arms), and you won't be able to move. You won't like it. The holding chair is no fun."

6 After quickly modeling the chair procedure (using tangible rewards as needed to regain the child's attention), the child should then rehearse going to time-out (explanation and modeling alone should be used when children refuse to rehearse even when given incentives). Here's an example of rehearsal: "Do you want a Sweettart? Then show me how you walk to time-out like a big boy. You are not in trouble. We are just practicing. Good job of walking to time-out all by yourself. You get a piece of candy for that. Now, when you're in time-out, how quiet do you have to be? Quiet like a mouse. If you get out of the chair, you will have to go over here to the holding chair. Sit in the holding chair and I'll give you a sticker. Good listening. Here's your sticker. Now, if you jump out of time-out, I will cross your arms like this and hold you in this chair. This is no fun. You won't like being held this way. So, show me how you can sit like a big boy in the time-out chair so I won't have to hold you. Good sitting. Which do you want, a sticker or a Sweettart? You were a good listener. Now we can play what you want to play."

7 For five- to seven-year-olds, the explanation of rules often involves devising a behavioral contract. At the beginning of the session, parents are coached in how to develop a list of privileges that can be restricted should the child refuse to stay in time-out. The child is encouraged to participate by helping to generate privileges and by signing the final contract.

8 For therapists using spanking as the backup for time-out escape, a demonstration of the spank is provided to the children. Sitting in the time-out chair, the parent explains that if the child gets out of time-out like this (stands), the parent will have to spank the child. Without actually involving the child, the parent acts out the process using gestures. For example, the parent mimics putting the child

across his or her lap and says, "I will put you over my knee like this, pull your pants down, and spank your bottom like this" (Then, the parent will demonstrate the spank using his or her own forearm). See Chapter 5 for a discussion of the limitations and ethical issues in the use of physical discipline.

GENERAL GUIDELINES FOR COACHING DISCIPLINE SKILLS

In learning to coach the discipline skills, it is helpful for therapists to understand how the parent feels during these sessions. Nervousness is common in the first discipline session. Parents may be concerned that they will do or say something wrong, that the child may become aggressive, that the program may not work for their child, or that they may not have the psychological strength to succeed. To provide consistent and controlled discipline procedures in stressful circumstances, parents need a calm, confident, and decisive therapist.

As the therapist, you may not feel very calm, confident, and decisive. Even though we have treated hundreds of families, we continue to feel some anxiety when taking the microphone for the first discipline coaching session. This anxiety is normal and natural. In many ways, a moderate level of anxiety is beneficial in that it helps therapists to prepare for the worst and react quickly to the inevitable dilemmas that occur during discipline coaching. Nevertheless, while it is normal to feel nervous, the therapist still has a responsibility to the family to project competence and control.

The most common mistake of novice coaches is to allow the parents too much latitude. Unlike the coaching provided in the play therapy portion of the program, the discipline coaching is extremely directive. In the beginning, the therapist should guide nearly every word the parent says. Otherwise, opportunities arise for parents to fall back into old habits, such as giving repeated instructions, using negatively stated instructions, using suggestions instead of direct commands, arguing or pleading with the child, and responding too slowly. A good discipline coach will actively direct the parents regarding when to talk, when to be quiet, when to look the child in the eye, when to ignore the child, when to walk, when to move quickly, and when to carry the child. As the discipline program progresses, parents will be able to conduct the skills with much less direction from the therapist.

In order to be active and directive in coaching, the therapist will provide numerous instructions to parents. A good rule of thumb for therapist-coaches is to incorporate the guidelines provided in the "Giving Good Directions" handout (see Appendix). The therapist should be giving instructions to parents in much the same way that the parents are giving instructions to the children. In general, coaching should be directive, concise, clear, specific, positive, and respectful. Guidelines for coaching discipline skills are presented in Table 6-1.

Table 6-1. Therapist Guidelines for Discipline Coaching

Project confidence and decisiveness
Be active and directive
Give only one instruction at a time
Tell the parents what TO DO (avoid "no," "don't," and "stop")
Coach nonverbals, as well as verbals
Use ample praise, particularly when parents follow instructions
Provide constant reassurance
Use a "running commentary" or "constant talking" approach to distract parents during conflictual situations
Include relaxation techniques, such as deep breathing
When parents become agitated, use a coaching voice that is softer and more monotone, with a very even rate of speech
When appropriate, incorporate humor to defuse tension
Make quick decisions when questionable circumstances arise

Give One Instruction at a Time

Like the parent, the coach should give only one instruction at a time. This helps parents to clearly understand what is being taught. A lengthy string of instructions such as the following would inevitably lead to parental mistakes: "Go ahead and get two blocks off of the table. Maybe the red and green one and then tell him that you need some help and that he needs to put the two blocks together for you." When given these instructions, the parent is likely to either leave out a step or insert a bad habit such as using an indirect command. A better approach is to break the instruction into smaller parts: "I'd like for you to prepare for the next instruction. Get the red and green blocks off of the table. Good job of getting ready. Now say, 'I need some help.' You gave a good reason there. Now say, 'Please put these blocks together.' Nice direct command."

Use Positively Stated Instructions

Also like the parent, the therapist should avoid negatively stated instructions. When a parent makes a mistake, such as getting enticed into an argument, the therapist should avoid saying things like "Don't argue" or "No talking." These negative instructions come across as critical and can damage rapport. In addition, negative instructions are limited in their effectiveness because the parent learns only what "not to do" rather than what "to do." Here is an alternative response to the parent who is arguing with the child: "Try to stay quiet right now. That's it. Just ignore her attempts to argue. Good job of ignoring. By staying quiet, you are letting her know that you will not give negative attention in the form of an argument."

Table 6-2. Sample Coaching Statements Addressing Parental Skills and Demeanor

---

"Nice job of staying calm."

"I like that neutral tone of voice."

"Good job of getting her to time-out like a robot . . . no yelling, no extra words, no begging. You got her there quickly and in a boring and routine fashion."

"Nice firm two-choices statement."

"Go ahead and take a couple of deep breaths. You deserve a break right now."

"It was difficult getting her to time-out. But, you did a great job of staying in control."

"I like how quickly you moved. That gives a message to him that you feel confident and in control, even if you don't exactly feel that way right this minute (said with humor)."

"That's just the way we like to see children taken to time-out . . . no extra attention. I think you've really got the hang of this."

Coach Both Verbal and Nonverbal Communication

The coach should keep in mind that he or she is coaching nonverbal as well as verbal communication. The coach not only is offering the parent specific words to repeat, but also is instructing them on movement, carries, physical proximity, touches, and timing. The coach is also responsible for cuing parents on when to stay quiet and when to ignore. In disciplining a child, facial expression, voice tone, and body language are at least as important as the words that are used. The coach can assist parents in giving enthusiastic attention to positive behavior (e.g., "You must be so proud of him! How about giving him a big labeled praise for minding?"). When inappropriate behavior occurs, the coach should encourage a confident and robotic approach (e.g., "Just ignore the bad attitude. Act like it doesn't bother you in the least. Now, say in a neutral tone of voice, 'You have two choices. You can either pick up the crayons or go to time-out.' "). See Table 6-2 for sample coaching statements addressing parental skills and demeanor.

Praise Parental Compliance

During discipline coaching, the therapist will give numerous instructions to the parents. We try to give parents a labeled praise each time they comply with the direction or prompt, even when all they do is to repeat our exact words. For example, the coach says, "Go ahead and give the two-choices statement," and the parent complies. We typically follow through by saying something like "Good, firm two-choices statement." The praises reinforce parents for complying with therapist directions and serve a teaching function by providing feedback on skills. Finally, they set a positive tone for the coaching. Parents feel good about themselves and the therapist when they are receiving a great deal of positive feedback. Examples of commonly used labeled praises include "good pointing," "nice enthusiastic labeled praise," "good job of restating that command," "nice job of staying quiet," "good idea to give a little hug just then," "good timing on the choices statement," "I like that ignoring," and "great job of staying calm."

Offer Support and Reassurance

Another major aspect of discipline coaching is reassuring and calming parents. As mentioned previously, parents experience a range of powerful emotions during discipline sessions. These emotions include fear (that they will lose control or their child will not respond), anxiety (that they will not perform well under pressure), anger (that their child's misbehavior is causing them so much stress), and guilt (that perhaps they are being overly punitive).

There are a number of components involved in reassuring and calming parents. First, it is important to remind parents frequently that the discipline procedures they are using are in the best interests of their child. It is natural for parents to experience doubts about whether they are doing the right thing when their child is crying, screaming, or saying "I hate you" while in time-out. A calming reassurance from the therapist, such as the following, can give the parent the strength needed to follow through during difficult moments:

> I know it is difficult to just ignore his cries. But, remember, you are doing the right thing. If he does not learn to accept limits and consequences now, he will have an even harder time when he enters school next fall. The first time-outs are always the most stressful. Soon he will be able to go to time-out calmly. He just needs to learn how. You are doing a beautiful job of helping him to learn to follow instructions. This will help him in school, with babysitters, with friends, and with relatives. He will be a much happier child because you had the strength to do what you're doing now.

Use Relaxation Training Strategies

As in the above example, often reassurances take the form of a running commentary. Not only does this distract the parent from anxious feelings and thoughts of quitting, but it helps to keep them focused on the goals. We have found that this technique of "constant talking" during stressful periods also has a very calming effect on the parents. In fact, we tend to adopt the soft, monotone voice styles used on relaxation tapes. When the parent's voice rises and he or she is escalating to an angry level, the therapist needs to assume an even quieter and more even rate of speech. In this way, the therapist's gentle coaching will help to balance out the parent's increasing agitation, helping both the therapist and parent to remain calm. Sometimes during the first coaching session, we use a more active relaxation intervention such as prompting parents to take deep breaths and coaching them through progressive muscle relaxation.

Make Use of Humor

Humor is another coaching technique that can help reduce parental anxiety and tension. Often during a particularly conflictual situation (e.g., ignoring a child who is tantruming on the floor), the therapist can defuse some of the tension by including a humorous comment in the midst of the running commentary. A smile or laugh shared between the coach and the parent can often help everyone to relax a bit. Here's an example:

> I know it's hard to ignore her when she's screaming on the floor like that. But, she is safe. I can see her just fine and she is not hurting herself. You can take a look out of the corner of your eye if you like. See, she is fine. She is used to people giving in to her when she throws one of these fits. Wonder what the people in the waiting room are thinking that we are doing to her! What they don't realize is what *she* is doing to *us*! Just joking. Glad you can still smile. You're really doing a great job of not losing your temper and not giving in. We will be able to distract her back to the table soon. Just keep ignoring and playing enthusiastically with the toys. By the way, I really like that unicorn that you just drew. I can tell you have a little girl who is into 'My Little Ponies.' OK, she's starting to calm down some now.

Make Coaching Decisions with Confidence

Many "iffy" situations arise that call for a coaching decision to be made quickly. For example, it is sometimes unclear whether a child has obeyed. The child may dawdle or act confused or comply with only a portion of the command. A rule of thumb for coaching is that it is more important to make swift, confident decisions than to try to ensure that each decision is absolutely correct. In fact, in many cases there is no "correct" decision. It simply involves a judgment call. One such "iffy" situation is when the parent blurts out an inappropriate instruction or two-choices statement. Sometimes it is best to go ahead and follow through with the discipline procedures in order to teach the child that the parent will be consistent. At other times, it is in the child's best interest to not follow through on an inappropriate instruction. In such cases, the parent can be instructed to pretend like that instruction was never given and continue with play therapy (e.g., "I think that it is too early in the coaching session to get into a conflict over writing his name. Just distract him by describing his play"). Again, the important thing is to act quickly and decisively. A long pause can cause everyone to become confused and provide an opportunity for the parent to make further errors.

THE FIRST INSTRUCTION

Once the time-out rules have been explained, modeled, and rehearsed with the child, the therapist coaches the parent in five to ten minutes of play therapy. The

Table 6-3. Sample Therapists' Instructions for First Discipline Coaching Session

Explanation	Instruction
It's time to practice following instructions.	Please hand me that stop sign (points and holds out hand to make it easy).
I could sure use some help.	Please put these two pieces together for me.
I'd like to see how good you are at puzzles.	Please try to put this piece in the puzzle.
Oops. A Lego fell on the floor.	Please pick it up.
We're going to practice minding.	Please write your name at the top of the page.
It's time to work on letters. This is a "B."	Please try to make a "B" just like mine.
Now we're going to play with a different toy.	Please put the cars over here (points to back of the table).
Our playtime is almost over.	Please put the crayons back in the box.
I'm worried you might choke on that block.	Please take it out of your mouth.
The rule of special time is that we have to stay at the table.	Please sit in this chair next to me.
It's almost time to go.	Please put one handful of Tinkertoys in the box.
You might fall.	Please get off the table.
I want to see how well you can follow instructions.	Please make a circle right here on the paper.

play therapy is designed to calm both the parent and the child. The child often feels bored and restless following the lengthy explanation of the rules. The parent, of course, is feeling anxious. After the play therapy has succeeded in setting a positive tone and calming everyone down (including the therapist), it is time for the first instruction.

According to the learning principles we are employing, it is best to start with small goals. This process allows the child to experience mastery before demands are gradually increased. A good initial step is to choose an instruction that the child is most likely to obey. If, for example, the child is already putting the pieces on Mr. Potato Head, the instruction could go like this: "OK, we're going to practice minding now (reason). Please put this ear on Mr. Potato Head (directive)." Similarly, if the child is working a puzzle, the next piece can be given to him or her with the instruction: "Please try to make this piece fit (directive)." The use of the phrase "try to" helps when giving an instruction that might present a developmental challenge. It lets the parent and the child know that our goal is not perfect execution, but effort.

Other first instructions that are likely to lead to success include telling the child to hand the parent a toy or to put two pieces together. For example, the parent could provide a reason such as "I need a dog for my farm." This can then be followed immediately by a directly stated "hand me" instruction such as "Please put the dog in my hand." Gestures will accompany the instruction to decrease ambiguity and help the child attend. Sample explanations and first instructions are presented in Table 6-3.

In most cases, children obey the first instruction. Then, the parent is coached to provide an enthusiastic labeled praise such as "Terrific job of listening! You did what I asked you to do, so you don't have to go to time-out. We get to keep on playing." This labeled praise serves several purposes: (1) it helps the child view following instructions as something to be proud of, (2) it increases the probability of future compliance, and (3) it reminds the child that new consequences are now in place for listening (praise, playtime) and not listening (time-out).

COMBINING PLAY THERAPY AND DISCIPLINE SKILLS

After the child has received praise for obeying the first command, parents are instructed to return to play therapy and to avoid giving further instructions for a few minutes. This play therapy serves to reinforce the child for compliance, decreases any anger resulting from being required to mind, and helps the parent remain calm. Every three to five minutes, another instruction is provided. In the beginning, the therapist tells the parent exactly what words to say. The parent's only responsibility is to repeat what the therapist suggests. Here is an example of how the therapist alternates between coaching the play therapy and discipline skills:

Therapist: "Good describing. You're helping him to stay focused."

Child: "My Potato Head has glasses."

Parent: "Yes, he has green glasses."

Therapist: "Nice reflection. That lets him know that you're really interested in what he has to say."

Parent: "I like the way you shared the glasses with me. If you share like that at school, you'll have lots of friends."

Therapist: "Excellent idea for that labeled praise. That's going to have a good impact on his social skills. OK, I think we're ready to move on to another instruction. Give him the reason first. Say, 'I can't see the picture on the box very well.' "

Parent: "I can't see the picture on the box very well."

Therapist: "Good reason. Now say, 'Please put the box over here so I can see it.' "

Parent: "Please put the box over here so I can see it."

Therapist: "Now, try not to say anything else. Just point. Give him time to obey. Good job of staying quiet."

Child: "Here's the box."

Therapist: "Say, 'Good listening! When you mind, you don't have to go to time-out. I'm so proud of you for learning to follow instructions.' "

Parent: (repeats labeled praise)

Therapist: "Go ahead and let him play what he wants to play and just use your play therapy skills. Good job of putting him back in the lead."

GRADUALLY INCREASING THE DEMANDS PLACED ON THE CHILD ————

According to the PCIT model, parents will learn skills more readily if they are able to practice the skills while receiving feedback from a coach. During the first discipline coaching session, the ideal situation is for the family to have a successful time-out under the therapist's guidance. Otherwise, the parents are left on their own for time-outs at home. When unsupervised, parents can easily make critical errors during time-out that can seriously interfere with the progress of the discipline program.

In most cases, a time-out is achieved in the first discipline coaching session. However, sometimes children will be 100% compliant during minding exercises which they may view as a "fun game." The likelihood of a time-out is increased when commands of increasing difficulty are provided throughout the session. Examples of situations that tend to elicit noncompliance include the following:

1	Switching from a more preferred to a less preferred activity
2	Giving cleanup commands
3	Using "real-life" instructions for naturally occurring events (e.g., child who throws toy on the floor is expected to pick it up; child who leaves the table is instructed to return; child who is sitting on knees in chair is instructed to sit on bottom; child who bangs a toy roughly is asked to play gently with the toy; child who has trouble sharing is instructed to share)
4	Leaving the door to the coaching room open so that the child may attempt to exit without parental permission
5	Moving to the playground, a conference room, or a more stimulating playroom to set the stage for more "real-life" instructions (e.g., putting toys away when finished playing with them, parking tricycles, leaving equipment alone)
6	Walking around the building to simulate a more "real-life" situation (commands include taking parent's hand, walking instead of running)
7	Increasing the pace of the instructions

Although having the opportunity to coach a time-out during the first discipline coaching session is ideal, we do not recommend that therapists push children to unreasonable limits to try to obtain a time-out. If a time-out does not occur, homework still can be given to most parents. For those less skilled parents who are unlikely to be successful at home without guided practice, homework can be postponed until further practice occurs in the clinic setting.

COACHING A TIME-OUT

Acting-out young children can engage in many unexpected behaviors when disciplined. The therapist must react quickly to novel situations, giving brief and. understandable instructions to the parent (see Table 6-4). Here is a common coaching sequence:

> Therapist: "Go ahead and hold up your two fingers. Good. Say, 'You have two choices. You can either hand me the block or go to time-out.' "

> Parent: "You have two choices. You can either hand me the block or go to time-out."

> Therapist: "Hold out your hand to make it easy for her. Point. That's it. One thousand one, one thousand two, one thousand three. She has not responded. Go ahead and stand up quickly. Take her by the hand. Start walking to time-out."

> Child: (sits on the floor)

> Therapist: "She's not walking. Pick her up quickly. Say, 'You didn't choose to mind so you have to sit on the chair.' "

> Parent: "You didn't choose to mind so you have to sit on the chair."

> Therapist: "Put her on the chair quickly. Good. Step out of arm's distance and say, 'Stay on the chair until I tell you to get off.' "

> Parent: "Stay on the chair until I tell you to get off."

> Therapist: "Now quickly walk away. Have a seat. Just ignore the crying. She's OK. Go ahead and take a couple of big breaths. You did a beautiful job of getting her to time-out quickly without giving any extra attention. Thirty seconds has already passed. Just two and a half minutes left to go. Good ignoring."

While sitting back at the table, the parent is instructed to organize the toys to make it easy for the child to comply. In the above example, the child was told to hand the parent a particular block. To set the child up for success, the parent can use the time-out interval to move all of the toys out of the way except for the one block. With fewer distractions, the child's potential for complying immediately following the time-out is increased.

GIVING PARENTS GREATER RESPONSIBILITY AS THE SESSION ADVANCES

As the session progresses, the therapist should allow the parent to become more independent in generating the discipline statements and determining the next step. For skills to generalize across settings, situations, and over time, parents need to learn to handle situations for themselves. Thus, too much dependency on the therapist becomes counterproductive. An example of how parents can be prompted rather than coached in the use of specific dialogue is as follows:

Therapist: "I think he's ready for another command. Go ahead and think of a reason and a command that you can give him."

Parent: "My car needs wheels. Would you please find me . . ."

Therapist: Interrupts and says, "Please find me . . ."

Parent: "Please find me some wheels."

Therapist: "Good direct command. Try to be quiet here. Give him a chance. Point to the wheels and point to your hand. Good waiting. He's dawdling. Go ahead with the warning."

Parent: "You have two choices. You can either find me the wheels or go to time-out."

Therapist: "Hold up two fingers. Now just wait. That was a good warning. Good neutral tone of voice. Looks like he's going to give them to you. How about a specific praise?"

Parent: "Good minding."

Therapist: (Prompts) "And when you mind you . . ."

Parent: "And when you mind you don't have to go to time-out."

Therapist: "Good job of praising listening. You also helped him to learn that, from now on, time-out and compliance are linked. OK, let's let him lead for awhile."

THE OPTION OF COACHING IN THE ROOM DURING A TIME-OUT

There are times during the discipline phase of the program when therapists may either (1) send a co-therapist or spouse into the coaching room or (2) enter the room themselves. The purpose of having someone enter the room during a time-out is to teach the child some of the time-out expectations while they are actually in that situation. It is inappropriate to look directly at the child during time-out and say things like "Time-out won't end until you're quiet," "Don't you dare get out of that chair," or "I don't appreciate that kind of language." Anytime the child is talked to during time-out, the latter loses some of its effectiveness because attention was given to the child. An alternative strategy is to send someone into the room to talk to the parent, not the child. The child then can learn about time-out from what is being said without receiving any direct attention.

Topics discussed in the room with the parent while the child is sitting in time-out may include the following: requirement for quiet; time-out continues for three minutes; child must agree to mind before time-out can end; child is not allowed to escape from time-out; predetermined backup for getting out of time-out; and how well the child is sitting in time-out. At no time is the parent, spouse, or therapist to look at or talk directly to the child.

This technique is based on the principle that children learn not only from being given the rules ahead of time, but also by going through the process. In our experience, children listen to the adults' conversation and learn many of the rules vicariously without actually having to test them. The conversation between the adults also helps reduce impulsive behaviors that are most likely to occur during the first few time-outs. A child who is about to jump out of time-out will think twice on hearing the adults discuss the backup consequence for getting out of the chair. Similarly, a screaming child often can be distracted into silence when another person enters the room.

The goal of this technique is to provide impulsive and aggressive young children with a mastery experience. If they can remain in time-out the first time or two, they learn that they are able to handle time-out. They also can learn that when they are able to sit for the entire three minutes, parents will follow through with the promise of giving them another chance to comply. Successful time-outs can then build on each other. Following is an example of how a spouse (or co-therapist) can be sent into the room to review the rules while the child listens from time-out (again, no attention is given directly to the child):

Spouse: "What's going on with Allen?"

Parent: "We were practicing minding and he did not write his name quickly enough. So, he had to go to time-out."

Spouse: "How long will he have to stay there?"

Parent: "Only three minutes. But, I can't let him out until he is quiet like a mouse. That's the rule."

Spouse: "So, you're waiting for Allen to get quiet so he can come out of time-out?"

Table 6-4. Sample Coaching Statements during a Time-out

"Just ignore that. He's trying to get your attention. Good job of showing no expression on your face."

"Try to watch him out of the corner of your eye. That's it. Now you can see him without getting any eye contact."

"I like how quickly you moved. You made a quick decision and got him to time-out before he had a chance to resist."

"I'm watching him very closely. It's OK if he bangs the back of the chair a little. If it looks like it's getting dangerous, I'll have you walk over and give him a warning."

"I know it's hard to ignore the crying. But you're doing the right thing for him. Just hang in there. Once this is all over you'll be surprised how quickly the anger goes down and the close feelings return."

"You can shake your head yes or no. Are you doing all right? I know it was hard to ignore him when he kicked you. But you did the right thing. You didn't let him know that it bothered you and you kept moving him to time-out. Wonderful job of handling a tough situation."

"That's it. Just play with the toys, and watch her out of the corner of your eye. Good ignoring."

"Try and keep a 'robot face.' I know some of the things he is saying are cute. But this is very serious. You have to be careful not to laugh because he will view this as a silly joke. Good ignoring."

"I'm timing. Looks like one minute is down and we still have two more to go."

"We're looking for five continuous seconds of silence. With all the screaming, it's going to be tough to get all five seconds. So, when we get close to five, get ready to move quickly to the chair. One thousand one (child screams). One thousand one, one thousand two, one thousand three, get ready, and go quickly. Say, 'Now that you're quiet, are you ready to pick up the crayons?' Hold your hand out to see if he'll take it."

"He's scooting the chair. Walk over quickly. Say, 'You're scooting the chair. If you scoot the chair again, I will hold you in the holding chair.' Push the chair back to where it was. Now say, 'Stay on the chair until I tell you to get off.' "

"She's looking like she's getting antsy. I don't think she can make an entire three-minute time-out. Let's see if we can catch her before she jumps. It would be nice if she could have a successful first time-out. She's quiet. So, walk over quickly and say, 'Since you're quiet and sitting all by yourself, are you ready to come hand me the block now?' "

Parent: "That's right, he has to be quiet. Also, Allen is not allowed to get out of time-out until I tell him to. If he gets up, I will have to take him to the time-out room. He won't like that."

Spouse: "That's good that Allen is staying in time-out so he doesn't have to go to the time-out room. The time-out room is no fun."

For safety purposes, there are other situations that may call for the therapist to enter the room. These include: (1) when a child repeatedly refuses to stay in time-out and needs to receive backup consequences such as a hold, movement to a time-out room, spanking, or restriction of privilege; (2) when a parent appears to be losing control or is close to giving in to the child; (3) when a child's behavior is completely out of control and the parent needs help in calming the child; and (4) when a child has become so aggressive that the parent cannot safely handle the behavior alone. In all of these situations, the therapist can provide a calming influence. On rare occasions, therapists who are certified in physical restraint procedures may choose to assist physically, to reduce potential danger to both the parent and the child.

DEBRIEFING FOLLOWING THE SESSION

Most parents need to debrief after the first discipline coaching session. Whether or not a time-out was needed, parents experienced some degree of stress during the session and may need to talk about feelings and concerns. The therapist can take this opportunity to praise parents for their perseverance and determination. Parents also can be specifically praised for skills that they implemented well (e.g., ignoring foul language, moving quickly and confidently, controlling their tempers). Through the positive feedback, parents can begin to see themselves as having the ability to be effective limit-setters for their children.

During debriefing, particular emphasis is placed on the "learning curve." Parents are given examples of how the child learned as a result of the explanations, modeling, role-playing, and consequences. For instance, almost all children learn that the two-choices statement is a firm limit, not an idle threat. Their increased compliance to the two-choices statement can be pointed out to parents who may not have noticed.

For parents who had a difficult session, the therapist should reassure them that time-outs will become much easier in the future. In fact, once the child begins to accept that the parent will be consistent in following through on the two-choices statement, relatively few time-outs will be necessary. The disruptive time-out behaviors, such as screaming, crying, and escaping, will improve as the child gains more time-out experience. For families who have easy first discipline sessions requiring no time-outs, therapists should remind them that all sessions may not go as smoothly. Therefore, they need to continue looking over the discipline handout and rehearsing their time-out skills so that they can be prepared when their child eventually does test the limits.

Finally, parents benefit from being reminded that being a consistent and fair disciplinarian does not cause harm to the parent–child relationship. Examples can be provided regarding how the child's anger was reduced by the play therapy or how the child quickly became engaged with the parent again after time-out. It is important for parents to realize that limit-setting does not have an adverse effect on children. In fact, it makes children and parents even closer. Children feel safe and comforted by parents who are fair and predictable. It is not uncommon during the first discipline coaching session to hear children say things like "I minded and I didn't have to go to time-out!" These statements are reviewed with parents as indicators that the child appreciates structure and is developing a more positive self-image.

Therapists may also choose to debrief with the child at the end of the session either individually or with the parent present. Positive behaviors should be reviewed with the child (e.g., staying in time-out without escape, being quiet in time-out, complying with directives, agreeing to mind after time-out). The homework assignment (described below) should be explained to the child. Sometimes role-plays are used to assist the child in learning rules and time-out expectations.

HOMEWORK

Throughout PCIT, homework is provided only when the therapist expects that both the parent and child can be successful with the assignment. If an overly advanced homework assignment is given and failure occurs, much progress is lost. So, an attempt is made to provide homework assignments in a graduated fashion so that the family can obtain mastery of each step along the way.

The homework assignment following the first discipline coaching session involves conducting minding exercises at home for ten minutes each day. The first five minutes should consist exclusively of play therapy. The next five minutes should involve the type of alternation conducted during the session: play therapy, directive, play therapy, directive, play therapy. The table and time-out chair(s) should be set up exactly as in the clinic. Also, just as in the clinic, the rules and consequences should be explained, modeled, and practiced. Parents are told to do the minding exercises at a time when they are not in a hurry. If the child goes to time-out, the ten minutes could easily turn into a twenty-minute commitment.

Not all parents should be given this discipline homework assignment. Those families who are not ready to begin discipline procedures at home will continue with the homework assignment of providing five minutes of daily play therapy. There are three general guidelines for determining whether homework should be given. First, if a "clean," uncomplicated time-out occurred in the clinic setting and the parent appears competent to employ the skills at home, homework should be given. In contrast, if the child was extremely resistant or aggressive during coaching, a second time-out under therapist supervision is advisable before sending the parent home to carry out the program independently. Second, if the parent has demonstrated the skills and judgment to perform the technique without therapist intervention, homework can be given. In contrast, if the therapist perceives that the parent will either conduct the time-out procedure inappropriately or potentially lose control and hurt the child during time-out, additional supervision is advised before giving a time-out homework assignment. And third, if no time-out occurred during coaching, but the parent has good discipline skills and the child demonstrated a learning curve during the session, a homework assignment can be given.

In preparing parents for the homework assignment, we anticipate how the child may respond to minding exercises. Some children quickly comprehend and accept what they perceive as the minding "game." They seldom require a time-out during minding practice. Yet, they still have significant compliance and attitude problems outside of the ten-minute homework period. If the therapist does not prepare the parents for this response, they may perceive that the program is not working. Optimally, parents should be told ahead of time that the goal for this week is to teach the child to comply at a high rate during minding exercises only. Compliance improvements outside of the ten minutes are not yet expected. Nevertheless, the following benefits of successful minding exercises should not be overlooked: (1) the child begins to perceive minding as fun and rewarding, (2) the child's habit of disobeying all instructions is being reversed, (3) the child's self-image is changing to that of a well-behaved child who likes to be helpful, and (4) the child learns that the parent will be fair and consistent in following through with time-out for noncompliance. Anticipating that parents will become impatient with minding exercises, the therapist should obtain a firm commitment that they will not endanger the success of the program by using the time-out chair outside of the ten-minute homework period. For the rest of the day, parents are encouraged to use any safe discipline strategy of their choosing, except for time-out in a chair.

A second possible response to minding exercises is extreme resistance. Some children will accept the rules and limits within the structured clinic setting, but then defiantly test the parents when the therapist is not present. Parents should be advised to stop the homework assignment and contact the therapist if any complications occur during minding exercises. Potential complications include refusal to comply with the original instruction even after a lengthy time-out, refusal to stay in time-out, or aggression during minding exercises. When the parent telephones, the therapist should obtain a detailed description of the events. If the parent used good skills and the child demonstrated a learning curve, the therapist may choose to have the family resume the homework. If, however, the parent seems unable to competently execute the discipline skills without therapist supervision, homework should be postponed until the family can receive additional clinic coaching.

Progressing through the Discipline Program

Helping families progress from the first discipline coaching session to the end of the treatment program involves the successive mastery of steps. On average, each of the discipline steps in Table 7-1 takes a week to master, and in two-parent families, approximately half of each session is devoted to coaching each of the parents. Some families progress faster than average while others require additional time. Both child and parental factors contribute to the amount of time needed for each step. For example, extremely defiant children may need more than a week for minding exercises, while children who are very active and disorganized may require extra work on house rules (i.e., rules for disruptive behavior). Parents who do not do their homework or who are inconsistent regarding the program will require additional sessions to master the steps. Other parental factors influencing the pace of the program include intelligence and their own parental role models. Parents with intellectual limitations and those who were raised by inconsistent, negativistic, or abusive parents tend to have more difficulty assimilating the skills. Thus, whereas most families spend a week on each of the discipline steps, this time line is reduced or extended to fit the needs of particular families.

Over the course of the discipline program, coaching becomes progressively less directive. As parents become more skilled, we recognize and reinforce their competency by giving them greater autonomy. A problem-solving approach is employed in which parents develop their own behavioral programs, evaluate the effectiveness of interventions, and make modifications as needed. In this way, we avoid fostering dependency. Our goal is for parents to have the confidence to apply their skills to new situations and problems by the end of treatment. This approach maximizes cross-setting generalization and maintenance of treatment improvements.

With children between the ages of five and seven, the therapist may choose to spend some individual time at the end of each of the discipline sessions. This is helpful for rapport-building, discussion of the child's thoughts and feelings regarding the discipline program, and preparation for the following week's homework. A goal of the individual time is to enlist the child's input and

Table 7-1. Progression of the Discipline Program

	Clinic procedures	Homework assignments
Step 1	Minding exercises with a few "real-life" instructions.	Minding exercises only (10 minutes/day).
Step 2	Minding exercises continue, but more focus on "real-life" commands (e.g., cleaning up toys, coming into the room when asked, taking parent's hand on walks).	Return to 5 minutes of play therapy with no commands. Enforce three to five carefully selected commands per day.
Step 3	Include siblings in session, if appropriate. Young siblings participate in minding exercises. Conduct school consult if needed.	Consistently use two-choices statement and time-out for all defiance to directly stated commands given in home. Continue play therapy.
Step 4	Siblings can again be included, if needed. Work with parents on managing all children simultaneously in "real-life" situations. Establish and enforce a clinic "house rule" such as "no hurting."	In addition to the use of time-out for noncompliance, consistently enforce one house rule in the home. Continue play therapy.
Step 5	Siblings may or may not be included. Focus on managing behavior in public.	Add one other house rule if needed. Public behavior assignment. Continue play therapy.
Step 6	Parents either come alone or with identified child only. Focus is on miscellaneous remaining problems such as bedtime refusal, finicky eating, soiling, self-stimulation, and social skills deficits. Any parental and marital issues not addressed by PCIT can be discussed in this session, and referrals can be made.	Specialized programs for miscellaneous problems (e.g., star charts, overcorrection, bibliotherapy, environmental manipulations). Continue play therapy.

assistance. Children are less resistant when they feel included in the decision-making process.

STEP 1: "MINDING EXERCISES"

The first step of the discipline program is described in Chapter 6. Emphasis is placed on the mastery of "minding exercises" both at home and in the clinic setting. Before a family can progress to Step 2, the following goals should be accomplished in both settings: (1) child is highly compliant with commands in a play context and generally demonstrates a good attitude during minding exercises, (2) parent is competent to give effective instructions and follow through consistently with the time-out procedures, and (3) child has learned to stay in the time-out chair. Impatient parents may pressure the therapist to move forward even though these goals have not been met. However, the therapist must be cautious in pacing the discipline program. If the expectations for the child are too high, the child can easily become frustrated and angry, which inevitably results in extra time-outs and even greater frustration. When parents are allowed to move forward without adequate skill acquisition, ingrained and ineffective discipline habits tend to resurface. A helpful intervention at this point is to remind parents that it took several years to develop these problems; "unlearning" these behaviors will take time as well. If parents move forward too quickly, they risk having the entire intervention fail. If they can be patient for another week or two, the child and the parents may have an adequate opportunity to master the discipline skills.

STEP 2: "REAL-LIFE" DIRECTIONS

The primary goal of the second step is to generalize compliance from a play context to more real-life situations. This is done by incorporating a number of "real-life" instructions into the clinic coaching. Typically, we begin the session in a childproof clinic room where both play therapy and discipline skills are coached. Then, at the halfway point of the session, we move the family to a more stimulating and chaotic environment (e.g., a large playroom, the playground, the waiting room, a conference room) which is more like the home environment. We have found that opportunities for "real-life" instructions are greatly increased when children with behavioral disorders are placed in less structured settings such as these.

Usually, this generalized or "real-life" coaching is not conducted via the bug-in-ear and occurs with the therapist in the room. The child is encouraged to play in a nearby area while the therapist and parent(s) talk about a number of issues (e.g., feedback regarding the coaching, school behavior, this week's homework assignment). A time-out chair(s) should be placed in an open area. On entering the new setting, the parent explains to the child that minding practice will be continuing in this room. While talking to each other, the therapist and parent watch for real life instructions to give to the child. For example, if the child continuously interrupts the adults, a directive can be given for the child to play on the other side of the room. When a child forgets to put something back in its proper place, a cleanup instruction may be given. As a bug-in-ear device is not being used, the therapist can whisper a prompt to the parent or write an instruction on a pad. After some practice, the therapist can point to something and the parent should have the skill to provide a well-timed explanation and a well-stated instruction. Other examples of directives that can be provided during this phase of generalizing from an analogue play situation to real-life experiences are listed in Table 7-2.

Table 7-2. "Real-Life" Instructions for Clinic Coaching

"Robbie, I need to talk to you for a minute. Please come over here."

"I'm worried you might fall. Please get down from that shelf."

"Running is not allowed in this room. Please go back and walk this time."

"I like it when you shut doors quietly. Please shut the door again, but gently this time."

"We're trying to talk. Please choose a quieter toy to play with."

"You need to stay in the room. Please come back inside."

"It's dangerous when you run away from me like that. Please take my hand so we can walk together."

"It's almost time to go. Please put your coat on."

"You left a toy on the floor. Please put it on the table."

"It's time to clean up. Please park the bicycle over there."

"That's dirty. Please put it in the trash can."

"I'm worried that you're going to break that record player. Please play with something else."

"Your shoelace is untied. Please come here so that I can tie it for you."

If a time-out is required, the therapist coaches the parent from within the room by giving prompts and phrases as needed. After time-out is finished, the therapist encourages the parent to provide a little extra attention to the child in the form of descriptions, reflections, and praise. This procedure serves as a good opportunity to discuss with parents the importance of reducing the child's anger level after consequences are dispensed. If attention is not given after time-out, the child may assume that the parent is angry with him or her. Hurt feelings and unresolved anger can lead the child to engage in behavior that could require another time-out. Just one minute of positive attention can eliminate most negative feelings and empower the child to display more appropriate behavior.

Homework Assignment. Toward the end of the session, the next homework assignment is reviewed. Because most families are not prepared to make the jump from enforcing compliance with commands during play activities to consistently following through on all episodes of noncompliance at home, an intermediate homework assignment is included in the program. The parent is instructed to give the child three to five "carefully selected" instructions each day. "Carefully selected" means that the parent has thought about the directive in advance, taken care to phrase it properly, and has the time and the energy to follow through with a time-out consequence if necessary. To help teach the child that minding practice and time-out are now occurring outside of the playtime, the parent will preface directives with this rationale: "We're going to practice minding now." This alerts the child to when noncompliance during the day will be consequated with time-out. After the preface, the parent will provide a carefully selected, direct command such as "Please put your socks in the hamper." If the child complies, an enthusiastic labeled praise is given (e.g., "I'm proud of you for doing what I asked you to do! You're learning to mind, and you don't have to go to time-out"). If the child does not comply, the parent makes the two-choices statement and enforces time-out if needed.

The "three to five instructions" homework helps to prevent parents from overusing time-out. If asked at this point to use the procedure for all instructions, all day long, parents are likely to become either inconsistent or overbearing. This step helps to ensure that there will be reasonable expectations for the child and that the child will not be sent to time-out too many times in one day. As always, parents are instructed to stop using the procedure and to call the therapist if a problem develops (e.g., aggressive outbursts, refusing to stay in time-out). Before ending this Step 2 session, the therapist and parent should generate a list of good instructions that may be used at home. Sample instructions for this week include the following: "Please put your shoes away," "Please pick up the clothes you dropped on the floor," "Please turn off the television," "Please brush your teeth," "Please put your coat on," "Please put your glass in the sink," "Please help me put the spread on your bed," and "Please put the dolls in your room." These instructions can be written on the top of the discipline homework sheet and a play therapy homework sheet also is provided.

At this point in therapy, parents may try to move ahead in the program prematurely. They often ask the therapist to suggest management plans for behaviors that are easier to deal with later in treatment. Examples include school problems, not getting along well with other children, public misbehavior, bed-wetting, profanity, and not sleeping in one's own bed. It should be explained to the parents that it is difficult to address these problems until the child is minding at an acceptable rate. Parents at this stage have their hands full with minding alone and would find it extremely difficult to be consistent with additional behavioral programs. Parents can be assured that if they persevere with the program and are patient, their concerns will be addressed in two or three weeks.

Families who continue to have difficulty with any of the Step 2 goals should remain at that level for an additional week. Factors to consider include whether the child: (1) complied reasonably well and did not require an excessive number of time-outs, (2) remained in time-out without escaping, and (3) displayed a positive attitude about minding. Parents should have good instruction-giving skills and should be fair and consistent in their use of time-out and play therapy.

STEP 3: APPLYING SKILLS THROUGHOUT THE DAY

Most families will be progressing nicely at this point in the program. In fact, therapists often enter Step 3 feeling as if there is little material for clinic coaching. Many parents have an excellent grasp of the play therapy and discipline skills, and children often comply nearly 100% of the time when provided with the two-choices statement. In such cases, the therapist can consider bringing a sibling into this Step 3 session, particularly if there is one within the two- to seven-year-old age range. The purposes of incorporating the sibling(s) are as follows: (1) to give the parent a consistent discipline plan that can be used with all of their age-appropriate children, (2) to teach the new rules to the sibling in a minding exercise format, (3) to make the work done in the clinic more generalizable to the home by having the parent's attention divided between the children, and (4) to provide more material to work with during sessions. Examples of issues that can be addressed when a sibling is present are provided in Table 7-3.

We commonly spend half of this Step 3 session in a structured coaching room conducting play therapy and minding exercises. The other half of the session is spent in a generalization environment with the therapist providing in-room coaching. When siblings play together in a room that has not been childproofed, there are abundant "real-life" opportunities for giving instructions, setting limits, using time-out as a consequence for noncompliance, and praising compliance. Often, the therapist will coach parents to use positively stated instructions to address negative behavior (e.g., instead of "Don't bang that block," say "Please put the block back in the toy box"). As always, the therapist may choose to reserve the last few minutes of the session for individual play therapy and rapport-building with the child.

Homework Assignment. The intensive minding practice in this session serves as much-needed preparation for the difficult Step 3 homework assignment. Parents are told to enforce all directly stated instructions given in the home and to provide a labeled praise each time the child minds. For noncompliance, they are to follow through with the two-choices statement, and enforce time-out if the child still does not comply. Occasionally, the parent may choose to preface instructions with "We're going to practice minding now" to help children remember that compliance is now a priority all day long, not just in minding exercises. As is the case throughout PCIT, daily play therapy practice continues at home.

In explaining this homework assignment to the parents, several issues should be discussed. First, the difference between direct and indirect instructions

Table 7-3.   Issues to be Addressed during Sibling Sessions

Turn-taking	Asking before taking toys
Sharing	Using polite manners
Getting along well with others	The "no hurting" rule
Alternatives to tattling	Problem-solving
Recognizing positive qualities of siblings	Keeping hands and feet to oneself

should be reviewed. Time-out will not be used for indirect instructions because they are stated in such a way as to suggest choice (e.g., "Could you hand me the remote control?"). At the same time, parents need to be careful about the types of direct instructions that are given. Because time-out must be used consistently for every act of noncompliance to a direct command, the number of direct commands usually needs to be drastically reduced. Otherwise, the child will be spending too much time in time-out.

Ways to prioritize and reduce instructions are discussed with parents. For example, we ask parents to suppose that their son has had a particularly difficult day. He has been extremely active, had a tantrum when left with the baby-sitter, continuously harassed the dog, and required three time-outs for noncompliance. It is dinnertime and the child is eating appropriately, but is sitting on his knees at the table. The parent is asked whether this behavior is important enough to warrant a direct command. During problem-solving, there should be a discussion of whether this behavior could be ignored in order to reserve the use of direct commands for higher priority behaviors (e.g., getting the child to come inside when called). It is up to the parents to prioritize which behaviors are sufficiently important to warrant a firm directive and the possibility of time-out for noncompliance.

The issue of disciplining under time constraints should be covered prior to this homework assignment. At this stage of treatment, we recommend that parents avoid the use of direct commands during transitional periods, such as when they are trying to get the child ready to go somewhere and cannot be late. The reason for this is that these transitional periods are high risk times for disobedience. Because the children may have not yet learned to comply at a high rate, the parents will often find themselves in the difficult position of either giving in to the child or being late for appointments. Instead of risking a confrontation, we ask parents to phrase their instructions as suggestions, which will not be enforced with a time-out consequence if the child disobeys. Alternatively, the parent may choose to do the task for the child to eliminate the need for a command. For example, suppose the family is late for church and Bridget has not yet begun to put on her shoes and socks. Rather than giving her a direct command, the parents may choose to either phrase the instruction indirectly ("Would you please put your shoes on quickly?"), or put her shoes and socks on for her. Parents often react to these recommendations with disappointment since most are eager to learn ways to deal with their children when they are in a hurry. Parents can be reassured that later in the discipline program their children will have overlearned compliance to such a point that direct commands can be given with confidence during transitional periods.

Parents must promise that they will not use time-out for anything other than disobedience of positively stated, direct commands. The discipline program will be seriously compromised if the parents begin to place the child in time-out for "being bad." The key to success in this stage is to use time-out only for non-compliance (i.e., refusing to do what one is told to do). Disruptive behaviors (e.g., hurting, profanity, attitude problems) will be handled later. To teach parents which situations time-out is appropriate for during the week, we often use this example:

> Suppose that on Sunday you wake up and discover that Brian has been up for quite a while. He has gotten into the refrigerator. He pulled out all of the eggs and cracked them open, one by one, on the kitchen floor. He also poured a jar of grape jelly into the middle of the scrambled eggs. When you come into the kitchen, Brian is sitting in the middle of the mess, finger painting with the mixture. Do you put him in the time-out chair? The answer is "no." You cannot use the time-out chair for this behavior because you have not given him a positively stated, direct instruction. You also have not given him a two-choices statement. For this week, you must promise me that you will not put him in the time-out chair without giving him the two-choices statement first. Now, if you can figure out a way to turn this into a minding issue, you can use time-out. What could you tell Brian "to do" that would make this a minding issue? That's right, you could tell him to take a rag and help you clean it up. Then if he refuses to help, you can give him two choices: to begin wiping up the mess or go to time-out. Can you see the behavior we are targeting this week? We can't send him to time-out every time he misbehaves this week because he would be in time-out too often. We have to start with one problem, just getting him to mind. Once he is following your instructions we will deal with all of the other problems. But, it's important that we do this only one step at a time.

The parents are given a discipline homework sheet and a play therapy homework sheet. We warn them that minding all direct commands is a difficult assignment for the child. It is not uncommon for children to develop a "bad attitude" about minding this week because it suddenly becomes apparent to them that the compliance expectation is no longer a game. Much testing of limits can occur. Parents are asked whether they are up for the challenge. If not, this assignment can be postponed while they do another week of three to five commands per day. If they are ready for the challenge, they are given the assignment, but are told to telephone the therapist and stop the program if they encounter serious problems (e.g., aggression, refusal to stay in time-out).

For children with continued behavior problems in the classroom, a school consultation can be scheduled. This is a good time to address school issues because the child is complying better and has learned to accept the two-choices statement as a firm limit, rather than an idle threat. Preschool and kindergarten teachers can be taught the use of effective instructions, labeled praise for minding, the two-choices statement, and the time-out procedure. In the classroom, coaching instructions can be provided to teachers by whispering prompts, providing suggestions during breaks, and writing phrases on a notepad. By adapting the home program to the classroom, the child quickly learns that there are minding expectations both at home and at school.

Depending on the family's success with Step 3, the therapist can choose to move forward in the progression or remain at this level for another week. Factors to assess when determining mastery include whether the child: (1) remained in time-out without escape, (2) did not require an excessive number of time-outs (i.e., fewer than four times per day), and (3) displayed a learning curve in that he or she developed better compliance toward the end of the week. Consideration should continue to be given to whether parents were fair and consistent in their implementation of the discipline and play therapy procedures.

STEP 4: HOUSE RULES

The primary goal of Step 4 is to teach parents to establish appropriate house rules. As a review, parents are reminded that children's behavior problems can be divided into two categories: failure to do what they are told to do (i.e., disobeying positively stated instructions) and doing things they are told not to do (i.e., breaking house rules). It is common for parents to enter Step 4 saying, "Yes, he minds when I hold up my two fingers, but..." indicating that a number of problems still exist. Examples of continuing problems include hurting others, minding with a bad attitude (e.g., cleaning up the toys by slamming them into the box), profanity, spitting, getting into off-limits possessions, and leaving the yard. Like noncompliance, the disruptive behaviors must be handled in a gradual fashion.

When a behavior problem is not amenable to improvement through the process of using positively stated commands for incompatible behaviors, the use of a house rule may be considered. For the first house rule, it is best to select a disruptive behavior that occurs with high frequency so that there will be many learning opportunities throughout the week. For example, some children jump on beds. Positively stated directives may be only partially effective in eliminating this behavior. A child may immediately comply when told to get off of the bed. A few minutes later, however, the misbehavior may be repeated. In such a case a "standing" rule called "no jumping on the bed" may be more effective than repeated "running" commands. Parents are asked to explain each new house rule to the child in advance, choosing a time when the parent is calm and the child is displaying appropriate behavior. A definition of the rule is provided at the child's developmental level. It is explained to the child that jumping on the bed can damage the bedding and will not be allowed. From now on, any time the child jumps on the bed there will be an immediate time-out and no warning will be given. Parents are instructed to use a three minute time-out and then to give a reminder of the house rule (e.g., "Your time-out is over now. Remember, no more jumping on the bed"). Unlike time-outs for noncompliance, there is no requirement that the child comply with the original command because no command was given.

House rules should be kept to a minimum (less than five). One reason for limiting the number of rules is to help ensure that time-out is not overused. Large numbers of house rules are associated with more frequent time-outs and increased frustration in children. Also, house rules should be enforced with 100% consistency. When parents develop many rules, their ability to enforce them consistently decreases. So, the therapist needs to work with the parent on determining which disruptive behaviors warrant house rules.

When deciding whether to employ a house rule, the first issue to consider is whether the problem could be handled effectively using a less restrictive strategy. We reserve house rules as a last resort. Strategies that should be attempted before implementing a house rule include the following: (1) selective ignoring, (2) strategic praise, and (3) using positively stated commands to perform incompatible behaviors. The second issue to consider is whether it would be possible to provide a consistent consequence immediately following each incidence of the misbehavior. House rules are only effective when they are enforced consistently. If the parent is unwilling or unable to place the child in time-out for nearly every infraction of the rule, the behavior should not be handled with a house rule. A third issue to consider is whether the misbehavior can be defined so clearly that the mother, father, and children can all agree about whether a rule has been broken.

To illustrate the decision-making process, we will consider the common preschool problem of whining. The first consideration is whether whining can be effectively handled with more positive strategies. One effective strategy is to offer a prompt such as "I can only understand you when you talk like a big boy," followed by ignoring of any whining. Strategic attention also can be used by taking special care to provide enthusiastic labeled praises when the child speaks clearly. The therapist may also review the "when...then" technique with the parents. This technique can be applied to whining as follows: "When you ask me like a big girl (boy), then I will give you the juice." The second issue to consider is whether it is appropriate or desirable to place the child in time-out each time a whine occurs. Given that whining is a developmentally normative behavior for very young children, many parents feel uncomfortable using time-out consistently as a consequence. Third, definitional issues should be considered. A careful definition of whining would be necessary to avoid confusion regarding whether a verbalization constituted immature speech, an expression of fatigue, or a whine. One option for defining the behavior would be for parents to label it (e.g., "That's a whine") for a short period prior to beginning enforcement of the "no whining" rule.

We reserve house rules for only a handful of disruptive behaviors. For aggressive children, a "no hurting" rule is usually necessary. We prefer the word "hurting" because it is easily defined and encompasses a range of aggressive behaviors (e.g., hitting, kicking, biting, pinching, hair-pulling). Profanity is another problem that may be appropriately addressed using a house rule. Although mildly offensive language such as "dummy," "I hate you," and "pencil-necked geek" can be managed through the use of selective ignoring and strategic attention, extremely offensive language may require a stronger consequence. In defining the "no bad words" rule, parents should carefully select a short list of profane words that no one in the family (parents included) is allowed to say. "Off-limits" house rules are particularly helpful for very active and impulsive children. Examples include "no getting into the refrigerator without permission," "no touching the computer," "no getting into mom's cosmetics and jewelry," and "no leaving the yard (house) without permission." Before resorting to an off-limits house rule, environmental manipulations should be tried such as placing cosmetics in a high cabinet. Other disruptive behaviors that may be appropriate for house rules include spitting, lying, stealing, and climbing on the furniture.

Each time that a house rule is introduced, the parent should provide both verbal and visual (e.g., illustrated "stop signs") reminders about the new rule. In addition, parents should make a special effort to praise the child for complying with the rule. For example, every thirty minutes to an hour, the parent should "catch the child being good" by saying something like "I'm proud of you for playing gently with your sister. You haven't hurt her this morning, so you haven't had to go to time-out." Using proactive steps such as these, many time-outs can be avoided.

During clinic coaching, one house rule (e.g., "No throwing") is established in the generalization room. Parents are coached to explain the rule and consequences, praise the child for complying with the rule, and quickly provide a time-out consequence if the rule is broken. At this point in treatment, all directly stated instructions in the clinic require follow-through with praise for compliance and the two-choices/time-out sequence for noncompliance.

Homework Assignment. The homework assignment for this session is to establish and enforce one house rule for a frequently occurring disruptive behavior. In addition, parents should continue to use time-out for all noncompliance to direct commands and provide daily play therapy sessions. In determining whether a family is ready to move on to Step 5, the following factors should be considered: (1) whether the child continued to comply at a high rate and did not escape from time-out, (2) whether the child demonstrated a positive response to the first house rule, (3) whether there is an absence of coerciveness in the parent–child relationship, and (4) whether the parents demonstrated appropriate use of discipline and play therapy skills.

STEP 5: PUBLIC BEHAVIOR

The major goal of Step 5 is to teach parents the use of discipline skills in public settings. The first half of the session is spent in didactic presentation, with the child playing quietly in another area. During the second half of the session, discipline skills are directly coached in a public setting. The particular public setting selected for coaching will vary depending on the physical environment and the needs of the individual family. Settings in which public behavior may be coached include the waiting room, the hallways of an office building, a hospital cafeteria, the parking lot where the family's car is parked, a nearby park, fast-food restaurants, department stores, shopping malls, and grocery stores.

It is helpful to begin the didactic portion of the session by discussing the thoughts and feelings that parents experience when their children misbehave in public. Many parents tell us that they feel intense embarrassment because they believe others regard them as incompetent parents when their children are disruptive. Some believe that their children are misbehaving so as to cause parental embarrassment. We find it helpful to confront these maladaptive cognitions by asking parents what they think when they notice someone else's child misbehaving. They typically respond by saying they feel empathy for the parent and that the child is probably misbehaving because of fatigue or hunger.

During the didactic portion of the session, parents are taught to apply discipline techniques they have already learned to public behavior problems. For example, both noncompliance and breaking house rules can receive consequences in public settings. To help children learn that "time-out can travel," we recommend that parents bring along a visual reminder that time-out is being used outside of the home. Parents can carry a time-out towel which can be rolled up and placed in a purse or shopping cart. Children are told that if they refuse to follow the rules in public, the time-out towel will be placed in an out-of-the-way spot and they will have to sit there for three minutes. To reduce the number of time-outs needed, parents should carefully prepare their children by explaining the rules and consequences before entering the public place.

Using a problem-solving approach, parents are encouraged to generate ideas for out-of-the-way places that may be appropriate for time-outs. Good options include dressing rooms, benches outside of stores, public restrooms, church hallways, and empty sections of stores. If the car is parked nearby, it can serve as a more private place for time-out, decreasing parental embarrassment.

During the didactic session, misbehavior in the car should also be addressed. Common behavior problems while riding in the car include taking off seat belts, kicking the back of the seat, yelling, and opening the car door. Safety permitting, pulling the car over for three minutes can be an effective time-out option. Children dislike the lack of stimulation involved in sitting in a still car. If other children are in the car, the parent can explain that one of the children is in time-out and should be ignored. To prevent boredom and associated behavioral problems in the siblings, the parent can talk, sing, and play games with the others until the time-out is over. If the parent is close to home, a two-choices statement can be given such as "You have two choices. You can either put your seat belt back on or you will go immediately to time-out when we get home."

For the coaching portion of the session, we meet the family in a preselected public setting. Parents are coached to state behavioral expectations and consequences clearly before entering the building. Once inside, the therapist-coach prompts the parents to use positively stated directives to manage child behavior. Examples of commonly used direct commands in public settings include "Please take my hand," "Please put your hands in your pockets," "Use an inside voice please," "Please put both hands on the shopping cart," and "Please stay in your seat." Parents may be coached to establish a standing rule for public behavior such as "no taking things off of the shelves." Running away is a common public behavior problem that is both dangerous and frightening to parents. Common strategies to eliminate this problem include overcorrection (i.e., requiring that the parent and child backtrack several steps and then walk together hand-in-hand), strategic praise for staying close to the parent, and giving positively stated incompatible instructions (e.g., "Please stand next to me"). Should the therapist need to coach a time-out, consideration must be given to parental feelings of embarrassment and strategies for handling onlookers who provide attention to the child. Although many parents feel considerable anticipatory anxiety about this session, by the end of the coaching most express surprise and pleasure at how few time-outs were needed in public.

Homework Assignment. The homework assignment for Step 5 is to practice discipline skills in public during two or three planned outings throughout the week. To set the family up for success, the outings should be conducted for the sole purpose of teaching the children that contingencies will be consistently enforced regardless of setting. The parent should not attempt to accomplish errands during these practice sessions as this could distract the parent from focusing on the discipline program. In addition to using the skills in malls, restaurants, and grocery stores, parents have the option of using a supportive friend's or relative's home as one of the places for public behavior practice. Parents may select another house rule to enforce at home this week and should continue to conduct daily play therapy sessions.

Factors to consider when deciding whether a family is ready to progress to Step 6 include: (1) parental comfort in using discipline skills in public, (2) child behavioral improvements in public settings, (3) child response to the most recent house rule, and (4) degree of improvement in the parent–child relationship.

STEP 6: REMAINING PROBLEMS

In Step Six, we address any remaining developmental problems. Because there is a high rate of co-occurrence between behavioral and developmental problems, many of the young children referred for PCIT demonstrate delays in speech/ language, motor, social, and self-help skills. When these delays are mild, several aspects of PCIT are useful for remediation. For example, research indicates that one of the best forums for stimulating language development is dyadic child-centered play (e.g., van Kleek & Richardson, 1990). Aspects of behavioral play therapy that may be particularly beneficial for language development include reflections with elaborations and developmentally sensitive descriptive statements. More severe developmental problems often require implementation of specialized programs. At this stage of treatment, we often design programs for elimination problems, bedtime refusal, pica, self-stimulation, separation anxiety, specific fears, social skills deficits, and food refusal. Whenever possible, we select empirically validated and behaviorally based interventions. Description of these programs is beyond the scope of this book, and the interested reader is referred to Lyman and Hembree-Kigin (1994) and Schroeder and Gordon (1991). For children whose disruptive behavior prevented them from participating in adjunctive interventions earlier in the treatment process, referrals can be made to allied professionals as needed. We commonly refer young children with developmental delays to physical therapists, occupational therapists, developmental pediatricians, speech/language specialists, and early intervention educators.

For several reasons, Step 6 is a good time to address individual and marital problems that were not apparent at pretreatment (e.g., depression, substance abuse, spouse battering). First, the rapport between therapist and parents is well-developed, making them more receptive to sensitive feedback. Second, parental stress has lessened as a result of child behavioral improvements, enabling parents to more easily focus on individual and marital adjustment. And third, maintenance of treatment gains could be compromised if individual and marital problems are not addressed. The therapist may choose to provide a brief intervention for specific parental problems. However, in many cases, we find it useful to refer parents for adjunctive treatments such as marital therapy, pharmacotherapy, substance abuse rehabilitation, individual psychotherapy, and support groups.

The Last Session: Posttreatment Feedback and Follow-up Planning

In PCIT, treatment is considered complete only when most or all of the presenting problems have been resolved or substantially improved. Once the therapist and family agree that this point has been reached, a posttreatment feedback session is scheduled. In this session, the therapist and the family review therapy progress, discuss strategies for addressing any remaining problems, and decide on a schedule for maintenance or "booster" sessions.

By the time PCIT is concluded, children's behavior is typically greatly improved and parenting stress is comparably diminished. In fact, some parents have difficulty remembering how distressed they were and how much difficulty they had coping with their child's out-of-control behavior at the time of the intake. Thus, major therapeutic goals for the posttreatment feedback session are to (1) help parents recognize the magnitude of progress made, (2) clearly link this progress to parents' consistent use of behavioral play therapy and discipline program skills, and (3) bolster the parent's sense of competence in dealing with problems that will arise after treatment is concluded. All of these goals help to promote long-term maintenance of parenting skills and improvements in child behavior.

RATIONALE FOR POSTTREATMENT EVALUATION

We always conclude PCIT with a posttreatment evaluation. In most cases, we repeat all of the pretreatment assessment procedures that were administered in the first session (see Chapter 2), including parent-report, teacher-report, child-report, and direct observation measures. There are several reasons for readministering the pretreatment assessment battery. First, it provides important information about areas of progress as well as remaining behavioral concerns that can be addressed during booster sessions. Most often, both parents and therapists are gratified to note clinically significant improvements from outside of normal limits to within normal limits on standardized measures of child and family adjustment such as the Eyberg Child Behavior Inventory, Child Behavior Checklist, and Parenting Stress Index. However, there are times when the posttreatment measures do not reflect the expected magnitude of progress. For example, parent-report measures may indicate that the child continues to display severe behavior problems, whereas parental comments and child behavior during sessions indicate much behavioral improvement. When discrepancies occur, it is important to identify possible causes. Sometimes, parents continue to report clinically significant problems on paper-and-pencil measures at posttreatment because they have become too dependent on the therapist and do not feel ready for termination. In other families, considerable problems still remain but have not been reported during weekly therapy sessions because the parent has feared "disappointing" the therapist. In both of these situations, termination of PCIT may be premature.

A second reason for readministering the pretreatment assessment battery is to collect data that may be used to generate a written report documenting the child's posttreatment level of behavioral and emotional functioning. In many cases, this is helpful in generating less restrictive preschool, day-care, or elementary school placements. A third reason for repeating the pretreatment assessment is professional accountability. Mental health practitioners are increasingly expected to document objectively the effectiveness of services rendered.

POSTTREATMENT EVALUATION PROCEDURES

The Dyadic Parent–Child Interaction Coding System (DPICS) observations are repeated at the end of the last discipline coaching session. As at pretreatment, we strongly recommend videotaping the DPICS observations so that behavioral changes from pre- to posttreatment may be directly viewed by the parents and child during the posttreatment feedback session. We conduct the DPICS observations exactly as at pretreatment, with one exception. In clinical usage, when we give parents the standard DPICS instructions, we add this instruction: "Use your best (behavioral play therapy, discipline program) skills in this situation." These instructions are added because some parents become confused about what they are expected to do and fail to demonstrate the skills they have performed so well during PCIT sessions.

At the end of the last discipline coaching session, parents are sent home with a packet of forms to complete and return to the therapist prior to the posttreatment feedback session. This packet includes the parent- and teacher-report forms that were administered at pretreatment as well as a parent-report measure of consumer satisfaction called the Therapy Attitude Inventory (TAI; Eyberg, 1992; see Appendix). The completed forms are collected prior to the posttreatment feedback session to allow sufficient time for scoring and interpretation.

PROCEDURES FOR THE POSTTREATMENT FEEDBACK SESSION

The posttreatment feedback session is a time for the family to recognize and celebrate their accomplishments in Parent–Child Interaction Therapy. They are told in advance that they will be reviewing their progress and will have a videotape show of "before" and "after" PCIT. The posttreatment feedback session typically requires one and one-half hours to complete. It is important that both parents and child attend. Even if one parent has not participated regularly in treatment, we typically extend an invitation to that individual to come to the posttreatment feedback. After preparing parents in advance for the content of the posttreatment feedback, we have on several occasions been asked if they could invite other family members such as grandparents or supportive friends to attend. Inclusion of nonparticipating spouses and extended family members in the feedback session can be quite useful for bolstering support for long-term use of the skills taught in PCIT.

Preparing for the Session

The therapist should bring to the feedback session a completed copy of the posttreatment evaluation report clearly documenting pre- to posttreatment changes, videotape segments strategically illustrating parent and child behavioral improvements, and any tangible rewards to be used as part of the termination ritual such as "Good Behavior Awards" for children and "Certificates of Accomplishment" for parents. The feedback session should be conducted in the playroom equipped with appropriate toys for the child to play with during adult conversation, and a VCR and TV monitor for playback of videotapes.

We preview pretreatment videotapes before the session in order to select approximately five minutes of tape to present to the family. When selecting segments, we typically look for good illustrations of the types of disruptive behavior that were of concern at pretreatment as well as examples of ineffective communication skills that were used by the parent. We also preview the posttreatment videotapes to select several minutes of contrasting child behavior and more effective parenting strategies.

For those parents who are particularly proud of having completed the full treatment program despite multiple life stressors, a "Certificate of Accomplishment" is highly reinforcing and an important termination ritual. For children completing therapy, we typically bring to the session a "Good Behavior Award" which takes the form of an inexpensive toy or special treat. An overview of the recommended steps for conducting the PCIT posttreatment feedback session is presented in Table 8-1.

Reviewing Treatment Accomplishments

While the child plays independently nearby, the therapist reviews with parents the initial presenting problems and then asks them to summarize their percep-

Table 8-1.	Steps for Conducting the PCIT Posttreatment Feedback	
Step 1	Ask parents to summarize their perception of major changes that have occurred in treatment and why	15 minutes
Step 2	Review changes on parent-report, teacher-report, and any child-report measures emphasizing the relationship between child improvements and parenting behaviors	15 minutes
Step 3	Show videotaped highlights of pre- and posttreatment observations and present "Good Behavior Award"	25 minutes
Step 4	Ask parents to specify remaining behavioral concerns and to problem-solve concerning the strategies they will use to work on these concerns	25 minutes
Step 5	Discuss a schedule for booster sessions	10 minutes

tions of the major changes that have been accomplished in PCIT. For each of the improvements noted, parents are prompted by the therapist to identify the reasons why these changes have occurred. Some parents have persistent difficulty associating their child's behavioral improvement with changes in their parenting strategies. For example, when asked to generate possible reasons for a shift from outside normal limits to within normal limits on oppositional defiant behavior at home, a parent may tell the therapist that it could have been the result of: (1) changes in the parent's work schedule, (2) a change in baby-sitters, or (3) enrollment in karate lessons. Although we acknowledge that young children's behavior is multiply determined, it is important that parents not discount the value of treatment. For parents to be sufficiently motivated to continue using their new skills over an extended period of time, they need to make the connection between consistent use of behavioral play therapy and discipline skills and corresponding improvements in child adjustment. As an additional method of reinforcing the changes observed by the parent, the therapist reviews pre- to posttreatment changes on norm referenced measures, noting the clinical significance of treatment effects. Throughout this discussion, parents are encouraged to turn to the child and provide enthusiastic and developmentally appropriate praise for behavioral improvements.

Posttreatment Video Show

Recognition of behavioral improvements is further solidified through the posttreatment video show. The video show is a powerful termination ritual. We frequently stop the videotape to allow parents and young children to discuss their reactions to what they are viewing. When viewing the pretreatment tapes, many parents express dismay at the ineffectiveness of their commands, limit-setting, and the overall negative tone of their interactions with their child. As mentioned earlier, by the end of treatment, many forget the severity of problems that brought them into therapy and seeing these behaviors displayed again strengthens their resolve to maintain treatment improvements. Young children may display a variety of reactions to viewing the pretreatment video and should be given a developmentally appropriate explanation of what they will see and why. Although most young children do not actually remember taking part in the pretreatment videotaping, they recognize that they are viewing themselves misbehaving. They may respond by making comments such as "I was a bad boy then, but not now" or they may appear to be embarrassed at their behavior. Parents are encouraged to discuss with the child sensitively the fact that they are looking at pictures from a long time ago, emphasizing the improvements in the child's behavior since that time. Next the posttreatment video is shown and both parents and the child are prompted to discuss the changes they notice from pretreatment. At this point in the feedback session, the therapist presents the child with a "Good Behavior Award" to reinforce further the child's behavioral accomplishments.

Reinforcing Competence to Handle Future Problems

For PCIT to have a long-lasting impact, parents must acquire the problem-solving skills to apply their new parenting strategies to a variety of problems that may come up as the child continues to develop. As parents progressed through the discipline program, they were given increasing responsibility for identifying problems, planning interventions, evaluating the effectiveness of their interventions, and making modifications in the interventions as needed. At this point in the feedback session, parents are asked to identify any remaining concerns, however minor, and to apply their newly acquired knowledge to form a plan for addressing at least one of these concerns. Although the therapist should facilitate this process by asking strategic questions, the goal is for the parent to be the architect of the plan. The therapist should then acknowledge the parent's expertise, expressing confidence in his or her ability to manage new problems as they arise. The following is an example of the way in which the "Socratic method" of asking strategic questions can be used to assist parents in problem-solving:

> Therapist: "What concerns do you still have about Johnny's behavior?"
>
> Parent: "Well, he does what I ask him to do, but he has started giving me a lot of back talk while he does it."
>
> Therapist: "Boy, I can see why you would be concerned about that. Can you give me an example?"
>
> Parent: "Last night, I asked him to put his dish in the sink. He did it, but all the way to the sink he griped about how unfair I was being because his two-year-old sister didn't have to do it. For 15 minutes afterwards, that's all he would talk about."

Therapist: "What strategies did you try to take care of the problem?"

Parent: "I tried to explain to him that his sister isn't big enough to clean up her dishes. He yelled at me, 'That's not fair! You're mean to me, and not her!' "

Therapist: "So you tried to use reasoning. How well did it work for you?"

Parent: "Not so great I guess."

Therapist: "What's your best guess about why reasoning didn't work?"

Parent: "I think in a way he liked the attention he was getting from me."

Therapist: "Bingo! I think you hit the nail on the head. He probably enjoyed your attention even though it was negative, and he probably continued arguing longer because of it."

Parent: "Well, what do you think I should have done?"

Therapist: "I think you know. I have confidence in your ability to figure out a very good solution to this problem. I know it's a lot easier to look back and think of solutions when you're not in the middle of a conflict. But I think it can be helpful to think about other ways to handle problems so that they will be easier to deal with the next time they come up. Looking back now, what other ideas do you have?"

Parent: "Well, I guess I could have just ignored it."

Therapist: "That's a good idea. Exactly how could you have ignored?"

Parent: "I could have just walked away."

Therapist: "How would you decide if ignoring worked?"

Parent: "If he quit arguing it worked."

Therapist: "What if he didn't quit arguing?"

Parent: "I guess I would have to do something else."

Therapist: "Is it possible that some good could come from ignoring that you might not be able to recognize right away?"

Parent: (thinking) "Maybe it would give him the message that I'm not going to pay attention to his arguing anymore so that he will eventually stop arguing with me."

Therapist: "You really have a good understanding of how to use ignoring! I remember how hard ignoring was for you when you first started treatment. It's true that when you first begin to ignore a behavior, it gets worse. But if you stick with it over time, the negative attention-getting behavior will stop. What would you do if he surprised you one night and took his dish away without arguing?"

Parent: "I would praise him."

Therapist: "What exactly would you say?"

Parent: "Thanks for putting your dish away without arguing and with a good attitude."

Therapist: "Terrific problem-solving. I knew you could figure out a good solution."

Scheduling Booster Sessions

Parents are asked to continue using their behavioral play therapy and disciplining skills for as long as is developmentally appropriate after PCIT is concluded. To enhance long-term maintenance of PCIT parenting skills and associated behavioral and parent–child relationship improvements, a schedule of "booster" sessions is developed. The number and frequency of booster sessions needed depend on a variety of factors, including (1) presence of impinging familial stressors, (2) degree of family and community support for using PCIT skills, (3) cognitive ability of the parent, (4) level of posttreatment skills mastery, (5) psychological functioning of the parent, and (6) parental dependency on the therapist. Although the schedule is developed collaboratively with the parent, on average we recommend that the family participate in one-month, three-month, six-month, and one-year booster sessions. During these sessions (usually scheduled for 90 minutes), parents are coached in both behavioral play therapy and discipline skills, and the therapist assists the parent in problem-solving regarding current behavioral and emotional concerns. A brief parent-report measure (e.g., Eyberg Child Behavior Inventory) can be completed to assist in tracking maintenance of behavioral improvements.

CONCLUSION

We hope we have succeeded in providing a practical step-by-step clinical description of how to implement Parent–Child Interaction Therapy. Although we are clinical researchers and included an overview of several PCIT treatment outcome studies in Chapter 1, we purposefully steered away from in-depth reporting of empirical findings. Nevertheless, we want to alert the interested clinician to the following set of additional PCIT readings which include both empirical findings and helpful clinical information.

Appendix

EYBERG CHILD BEHAVIOR INVENTORY

Rater's name: _____ Child's name: _____
Relationship to child: _____ Child's age: _____
Date of rating: _____ Birthdate: _____

Directions: Below is a series of phrases that describe children's behavior. Please (1) circle the number describing <u>how often</u> the behavior <u>currently</u> occurs with your child, and (2) circle either "yes" <u>or</u> "no" to indicate whether the behavior is <u>currently a problem</u>.

	How often does this occur with your child?						Is this a problem for you?	
	Never	Seldom	Sometimes	Often	Always			
1. Dawdles in getting dressed	1	2	3	4	5	6	7	Yes No
2. Dawdles or lingers at mealtime	1	2	3	4	5	6	7	Yes No
3. Has poor table manners	1	2	3	4	5	6	7	Yes No
4. Refuses to eat food presented	1	2	3	4	5	6	7	Yes No
5. Refuses to do chores when asked	1	2	3	4	5	6	7	Yes No
6. Slow in getting ready for bed	1	2	3	4	5	6	7	Yes No
7. Refuses to go to bed on time	1	2	3	4	5	6	7	Yes No
8. Does not obey house rules on his own	1	2	3	4	5	6	7	Yes No
9. Refuses to obey until threatened with punishment	1	2	3	4	5	6	7	Yes No
10. Acts defiant when told to do something	1	2	3	4	5	6	7	Yes No
11. Argues with parents about rules	1	2	3	4	5	6	7	Yes No
12. Gets angry when doesn't get his own way	1	2	3	4	5	6	7	Yes No
13. Has temper tantrums	1	2	3	4	5	6	7	Yes No
14. Sasses adults	1	2	3	4	5	6	7	Yes No
15. Whines	1	2	3	4	5	6	7	Yes No
16. Cries easily	1	2	3	4	5	6	7	Yes No
17. Yells or screams	1	2	3	4	5	6	7	Yes No
18. Hits parents	1	2	3	4	5	6	7	Yes No
19. Destroys toys and other objects	1	2	3	4	5	6	7	Yes No
20. Is careless with toys and other objects	1	2	3	4	5	6	7	Yes No

		Never	Seldom		Sometimes	Often		Always	How often does this occur with your child?	Is this a problem for you?
21.	Steals	1	2	3	4	5	6	7	Yes	No
22.	Lies	1	2	3	4	5	6	7	Yes	No
23.	Teases or provokes other children	1	2	3	4	5	6	7	Yes	No
24.	Verbally fights with friends his own age	1	2	3	4	5	6	7	Yes	No
25.	Verbally fights with sisters and brothers	1	2	3	4	5	6	7	Yes	No
26.	Physically fights with friends	1	2	3	4	5	6	7	Yes	No
27.	Physically fights with sisters and brothers	1	2	3	4	5	6	7	Yes	No
28.	Constantly seeks attention	1	2	3	4	5	6	7	Yes	No
29.	Interrupts	1	2	3	4	5	6	7	Yes	No
30.	Is easily distracted	1	2	3	4	5	6	7	Yes	No
31.	Has short attention span	1	2	3	4	5	6	7	Yes	No
32.	Fails to finish tasks or projects	1	2	3	4	5	6	7	Yes	No
33.	Has difficulty entertaining himself alone	1	2	3	4	5	6	7	Yes	No
34.	Has difficulty concentrating on one thing	1	2	3	4	5	6	7	Yes	No
35.	Is overactive or restless	1	2	3	4	5	6	7	Yes	No
36.	Wets the bed	1	2	3	4	5	6	7	Yes	No

SUTTER–EYBERG STUDENT BEHAVIOR INVENTORY

Child's name: _____   Child's age: _____
Teacher's name: _____   Child's sex: _____
Date of rating: _____   Birthdate: _____

Directions: Below is a series of phrases that describe children's behavior. Please (1) circle the number describing <u>how often</u> the behavior <u>currently</u> occurs with this student, and (2) circle either "yes" <u>or</u> "no" to indicate whether the behavior is <u>currently a problem</u>.

		How often does this occur with this student?						Is this a problem for you?	
	Never	Seldom	Sometimes	Often	Always				
1. Dawdles in obeying rules or instructions	1	2	3	4	5	6	7	Yes	No
2. Argues with teachers about rules or instructions	1	2	3	4	5	6	7	Yes	No
3. Has difficulty accepting criticism or correction	1	2	3	4	5	6	7	Yes	No
4. Does not obey school rules on his/her own	1	2	3	4	5	6	7	Yes	No
5. Refuses to obey until threatened with pubishment	1	2	3	4	5	6	7	Yes	No
6. Gets angry when doesn't get his/her own way	1	2	3	4	5	6	7	Yes	No
7. Acts defiant when told to do something	1	2	3	4	5	6	7	Yes	No
8. Has temper tantrums	1	2	3	4	5	6	7	Yes	No
9. Sasses teacher(s)	1	2	3	4	5	6	7	Yes	No
10. Whines	1	2	3	4	5	6	7	Yes	No
11. Cries	1	2	3	4	5	6	7	Yes	No
12. Pouts	1	2	3	4	5	6	7	Yes	No
13. Yells or screams	1	2	3	4	5	6	7	Yes	No
14. Hits teacher(s)	1	2	3	4	5	6	7	Yes	No
15. Is careless with books and other objects	1	2	3	4	5	6	7	Yes	No
16. Destroys books and other objects	1	2	3	4	5	6	7	Yes	No
17. Steals	1	2	3	4	5	6	7	Yes	No
18. Lies	1	2	3	4	5	6	7	Yes	No
19. Makes noises in class	1	2	3	4	5	6	7	Yes	No
20. Teases or provokes other students	1	2	3	4	5	6	7	Yes	No

		How often does this occur with this student?							Is this a problem for you?	
		Never	Seldom	Sometimes		Often		Always		
21.	Acts bossy with other students	1	2	3	4	5	6	7	Yes	No
22.	Verbally fights with other students	1	2	3	4	5	6	7	Yes	No
23.	Physically fights with other students	1	2	3	4	5	6	7	Yes	No
24.	Demands teacher attention	1	2	3	4	5	6	7	Yes	No
25.	Interrupts teachers	1	2	3	4	5	6	7	Yes	No
26.	Interrupts other students	1	2	3	4	5	6	7	Yes	No
27.	Has difficulty entering groups	1	2	3	4	5	6	7	Yes	No
28.	Has difficulty sharing materials	1	2	3	4	5	6	7	Yes	No
29.	Is uncooperative in group activities	1	2	3	4	5	6	7	Yes	No
30.	Blames others for problem behaviors	1	2	3	4	5	6	7	Yes	No
31.	Is easily distracted	1	2	3	4	5	6	7	Yes	No
32.	Has difficulty staying on task	1	2	3	4	5	6	7	Yes	No
33.	Acts frustrated with difficult tasks	1	2	3	4	5	6	7	Yes	No
34.	Fails to finish tasks or projects	1	2	3	4	5	6	7	Yes	No
35.	Impulsive, acts before thinking	1	2	3	4	5	6	7	Yes	No
36.	Is overactive or restless	1	2	3	4	5	6	7	Yes	No

DYADIC PARENT–CHILD INTERACTION CODING SYSTEM (DPICS)
CLINICALLY MODIFIED RECORDING FORM

Child's name _____   Observer's name _____

Parent's name _____   Date _____

Intake				Treatment sessions											Boosters			
A	B	1	2	3	4	5	6	7	8	9	10	11	12	A	B	C	D

Parent behaviors		Child behaviors
Direct command followed by . . .		No opportunity
		Compliance
		Noncompliance
Indirect command followed by . . .		No opportunity
		Compliance
		Noncompliance
Descriptive statement		Disruptive behavior . . .
		Ignored
		Responded to
Reflective statement		Other child behavior
Unlabeled praise		Clinical notes
Labeled praise		
Question		
Critical statement		
Other verbalization		

SUMMARY OF DPICS CODE DEFINITIONS

Descriptive statement: A declarative sentence or phrase that gives an account of the objects or people in the situation or the activity occurring during the interaction (e.g., You're building a pickup truck; You're sitting quietly).

Reflective statement: A declarative phrase or statement that immediately repeats the child's verbalization. The reflection may be exactly the same words the child said, may contain synonymous words, or may contain some elaboration on the child's statement, but the basic content must be the same as the child's message (e.g., CHILD: I made a big square. PARENT: You made a big square inside this big circle).

Unlabeled praise: A nonspecific verbalization that expresses a favorable judgment on an activity, product, or attribute of the child (e.g., Great; Nice; Good work; Perfect!).

Labeled praise: Any specific verbalization that expresses a favorable judgment on an activity, product, or attribute of the child (e.g., That's a terrific house you made; You have a beautiful smile).

Question: A descriptive or reflective comment expressed in question form. Some questions are differentiated from statements by voice inflection (e.g., That's the baby?).

Critical statement: A verbalization that finds fault with the activities, products, or attributes of the child (e.g., You're being naughty; That's a sloppy picture).

Direct command: A clearly stated order, demand, or direction in declarative form. The statement must be sufficiently specific as to indicate the behavior that is expected from the child (e.g., Put your hands in your lap; Please put that block here).

Indirect command: An order, demand, or direction for a behavioral response that is implied, nonspecific, or stated in question form (e.g., Put it here, OK?; Johnny!; Let's take out the red blocks).

Disruptive behavior: Any *cry* (inarticulate utterance of distress), *yell* (loud screech, scream, shout, or loud crying), *whine* (words uttered in a slurring, nasal, high-pitched, falsetto voice), *smart talk* (impudent or disrespectful speech, e.g., You're stupid; No!; I hate you; Why should I?; Oh, that's just great), *destructive* (destroys, damages, or attempts to damage any object, such as throwing blocks at wall; banging Lincoln Log on table; kicking toy box), or *physical negative* (bodily attack or attempt to attack the parent, such as hitting; slapping; biting; pinching; throwing something at the parent; kicking; pulling hair; twisting finger; standing on toe).

Ignores: Parent remains silent, maintains a neutral facial expression, avoids or breaks eye contact with the child, and makes no movement in response to the child, except to turn away.

Responds to: Any verbal or nonverbal reaction by the parent following a disruptive child behavior.

No opportunity: Child is not given an adequate chance to comply with a command (e.g., command is vague; behavior requested is not within the child's competence; parent quickly repeats a command; parent quickly issues another command; parent issues a command while child is already doing requested action; parent does the requested behavior for the child).

Compliance: Child obeys, begins to obey, or attempts to obey a direct or indirect parental command within three seconds (e.g., PARENT: Draw a person. CHILD: [immediately begins drawing a face]).

Noncompliance: Child does not begin obeying a direct or indirect parental command (e.g., ignoring parent; refusing to obey; countercommanding; making an excuse; arguing) within three seconds.

Adapted and reprinted by permission from Eyberg, S. M., & Robinson, E. A. (1983). Dyadic Parent–Child Interaction Coding System: A manual. *Psychological Documents, 13*, Ms. No. 2582. (Available from Social and Behavior Sciences Documents, Select Press, P. O. Box 9838, San Rafael, CA 94912.)

"Do" and "Don't" Skills for Behavioral Play Therapy—Parent Handout

Rule	Reason	Examples
Do **D**escribe appropriate behavior.	Allows child to lead Shows child you're interested Teaches concepts Models speech Holds child's attention Organizes child's thoughts about play	That's a red block. You're making a tower. You drew a smiling face. The cowboy looks happy.
Do **R**eflect appropriate talk	Doesn't control the conversation Shows child you're really listening Demonstrates acceptance and understanding Improves child's speech Increases verbal communication	Child: I made a star. Parent: Yes, you made a star. Child: The camel got bumps on top. Parent: It has two humps on its back. Child: I like to play with this castle. Parent: This is a fun castle to play with.
Do **I**mitate appropriate play.	Lets child lead Approves child's choice of play Shows child you are involved Shows child how to play with others (forms basis of taking turns) Tends to increase child's imitation of what you do	Child: I'm putting baby to bed. Parent: I'll put sister to bed too. Child: I'm making a sun in the sky. Parent: I'm going to put a sun in my picture too.
Do **P**raise appropriate behavior.	Causes the behavior to increase Lets child know what you like Increases self-esteem Adds to warmth of the relationship Makes both parent and child feel good!	Terrific counting! I like the way you're playing so quietly. You have wonderful ideas for this game. I'm proud of you for being polite. You did a nice job on that building. Your design is pretty. Thank you for showing the colors to me.

Rule	Reason	Examples
Ignore inappropriate behavior (unless dangerous or destructive) a. Don't look at child, speak, smile, frown, etc. b. Ignore every time c. Expect behavior to increase at first	Avoids increasing bad behavior Decreases some behaviors Helps child notice difference between your responses to good and bad behavior	Child: (Sasses parent, then picks up toy) Parent: (Ignores sass; praises picking up) Child: (hits parent) Parent: (GAME STOPS; can't be ignored)
Don't give *commands*.	Doesn't allow child to lead Can cause unpleasantness Child obedience will taught later	*Indirect* Will you hand me that paper? Could you tell me the alphabet? *Direct* Look at this. Please tie your shoe. Come here.
Don't ask *questions*.	Leads the conversation instead of following Many are commands or require an answer May seem like you aren't listening or disagree with child	That's a blue one, right? What color is this? Are you having fun? You want to play with the wastebasket?
Don't *criticize*.	Doesn't work to decrease bad behaviors Often increases the criticized behavior May lower the child's self-esteem Creates an unpleasant interaction	You're being naughty. I don't like it when you talk back. Don't scribble on your paper. No, honey, that's not right. That design is ugly.

Reprinted by permission from Eyberg and Boggs (1989).

SUGGESTED TOYS FOR BEHAVIORAL PLAY THERAPY—PARENT HANDOUT

Creative, constructional toys, like:
  Building blocks
  Legos
  Duplos
  Tinkertoys
  Magnetic blocks
  Lincoln Logs
  Constructo-Straws
  Mr. Potato Head
  Dollhouse with miniature people
  Bristle Blocks
  Toy garage with cars
  Waffle Blocks
  School bus with riders
  Erector Set
  Toy farm with animals
  Chalkboard and colored chalk
  Crayons and paper
  Magnetic picture board

TOYS TO AVOID DURING BEHAVIORAL PLAY THERAPY

Ones that encourage rough play, like:
  bats, balls, boxing gloves, punching bag

Ones that lead to aggressive play, like:
  toy guns, toy swords, toy cowboys and Indians, superhero figures

Ones that could get out of hand and require limit-setting, like:
  paints, scissors, Playdoh

Ones that have preset rules, like:
  board games, card games

Ones that discourage conversation, like:
  books, audiotapes

Ones that lead parent or child to pretend they are someone else, like:
  puppets, costumes, toy phones, dolls

BEHAVIORAL PLAY THERAPY HOMEWORK SHEET

DATE	(Did you practice play therapy for five minutes?) YES	NO	Note any problems that came up
MONDAY			
TUESDAY			
WEDNESDAY			
THURSDAY			
FRIDAY			
SATURDAY			
SUNDAY			

GIVING GOOD DIRECTIONS—PARENT HANDOUT

Rule	Rationale	Examples
Make commands direct, not indirect.	Eliminates any ambiguity about whether parent expects child to obey Makes it clear the child, not parent, is to do the task	Direct: Sit down right here. Indirect: Would you like to sit down? Direct: Pick up your toys. Indirect: *Let's* pick up your toys, OK?
Make commands single and small, not compound	Easier for child to obey smaller commands that are not overwhelming Some children can't remember multiple-part commands The child gets more opportunities for praise	Put your shoes in the closet. (instead of...Clean your room) Put on pajamas. Brush your teeth. Use the bathroom. (instead of...Get ready for bed)
State commands positively (tell child what *to* do, instead of what *not* to do).	Oppositional children rebel against "stop" and "don't" commands Tells child what (s)he can do instead	Child: (on kitchen counter) Parent: Get down please. (instead of...Don't climb on the counter!) Child: (bouncing ball indoors) Parent: Please get a book to read. (instead of...Stop bouncing that ball!) Child: (runs away from parent) Parent: Hold my hand. (instead of...Don't run away from me!)
Make commands specific, not vague.	Lets child know exactly what is expected Eliminates confusion Makes it easier to decide whether child has obeyed	Use your indoor voice. (instead of...Act nice!) Please walk (instead of...Behave yourself.) Wait for your turn. (instead of...Play nicely.)
Use a neutral tone of voice instead of pleading or yelling.	Children need to learn to respond to commands given in a normal, conversational voice Makes interactions more pleasant for both child and parent	Come sit next to me. (instead of...Sit here now!! or It would really make mommy happy if you would sit here, please?!)

Continued

Rule	Rationale	Examples
Be polite and respectful, while still being direct.	Makes interactions more pleasant Models good social skills Less likely to cause an oppositional child to disobey	Please hand me the crayon. Sit next to me please.
Save direct commands for things you're sure the child can do.	It's unfair to punish disobedience if the child was unable to obey To encourage a child to try something new, use an indirect command or suggestion, instead of a direct command	Make a picture. (instead of . . . Draw a stop sign) Would you like to try and sign it? (instead of . . . Write your name)
Don't give too many direct commands.	Neither adults nor children like to be told what to do constantly If parents give many commands, it is hard to follow through with consequences each time	
Always provide a consequence for obedience and disobedience.	Fastest way to teach young children to mind better Compliance should not be taken for granted Consistency in providing consequences is the most powerful tool for improving child behavior	Parent: Hand me your paper. Child: (hands paper to parent) Parent: Thanks for doing what I asked! You're a good helper. Child: (fails to hand paper to parent) Parent: You have two choices. You can hand me your paper or sit in time-out.
Use choice commands with older preschoolers.	Encourages the development of autonomy and decision-making Doesn't take the "power" away from a child who tends to get in power struggles	Please watch TV or color quietly. Please put on your white socks or your blue socks. Use your indoor voice or play in the backyard.

Continued

Rule	Rationale	Examples
Use explanations sparingly.	Children who ask for explanations are usually more interested in stalling than knowing the answer Gives child the impression that he might be able to talk his way out of it If used, give explanation before the command to head off arguing	Parent: Put the crayons away. Child: Why? Parent: Because we need to get ready to go. Child: After I finish. Parent: I said put the crayons away now!! Better... Parent: Our playtime is over and we need to get ready to go to the store. Please put your crayons away. Child: Why? Parent: (ignores delay tactics because explanation has already been given)

DIAGRAM OF DISCIPLINE PROCEDURE—PARENT HANDOUT

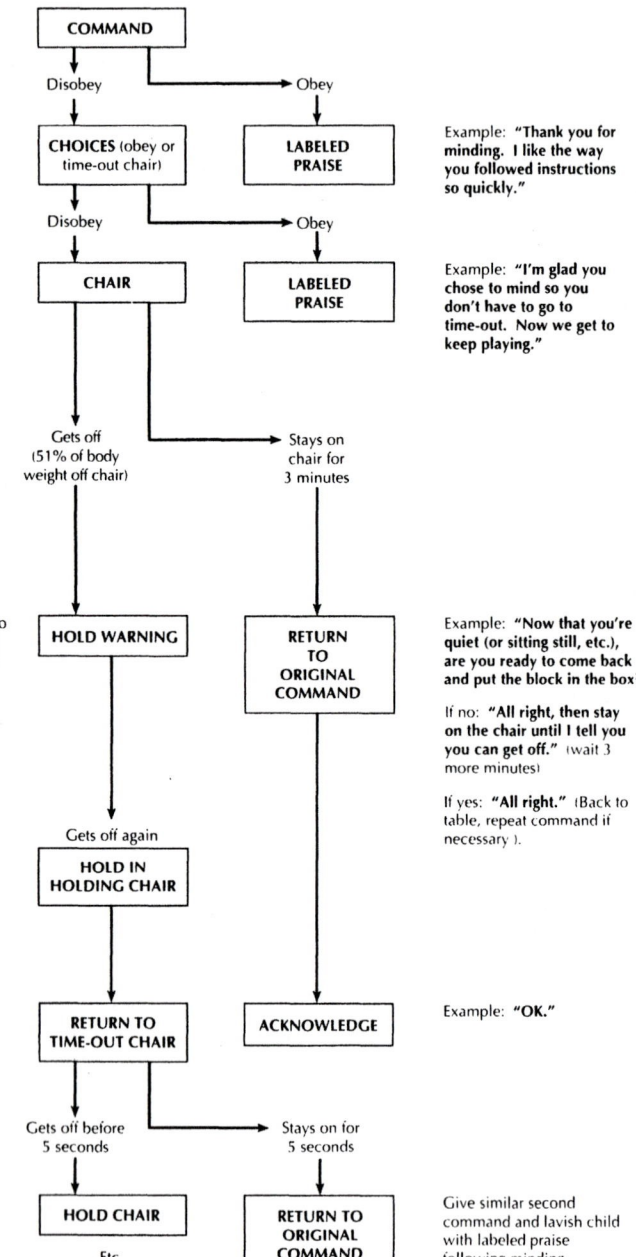

Explanation: **"It's time to go."**
Instruction: **"Please put the block in the box."**

COMMAND

Disobey → Obey

You have two choices. You can either _____ or sit on the chair."

CHOICES (obey or time-out chair)

LABELED PRAISE

Example: **"Thank you for minding. I like the way you followed instructions so quickly."**

Disobey → Obey

Stay calm. Stand up and take the child immediately to the chair as you say, **"You didn't choose to mind, so you have to sit on the chair."** Step away from the child quickly and say, **"Stay on the chair until I tell you you can get off."** Use a downward hand motion as you say this.

CHAIR

LABELED PRAISE

Example: **"I'm glad you chose to mind so you don't have to go to time-out. Now we get to keep playing."**

Gets off (51% of body weight off chair) → Stays on chair for 3 minutes

Take the child immediately back to the chair while saying, **"If you get off the chair again I will hold you in the holding chair."** (This warning occurs once for each time-out. Warnings also may be given for rocking the chair, scooting the chair, and standing up in the chair).

HOLD WARNING

RETURN TO ORIGINAL COMMAND

Example: **"Now that you're quiet (or sitting still, etc.), are you ready to come back and put the block in the box?"**

If no: **"All right, then stay on the chair until I tell you you can get off."** (wait 3 more minutes)

If yes: **"All right."** (Back to table, repeat command if necessary).

Gets off again

Take child back to chair while saying: **"You got off the chair before I told you you could so I am going to hold you in the holding chair."** (1st Hold = up to 45 seconds. 2nd Hold = up to 90 seconds. 3rd Hold = up to 3 minutes).

Example: **"You need to sit by yourself in the time-out chair like a big boy/girl."**

HOLD IN HOLDING CHAIR

RETURN TO TIME-OUT CHAIR

ACKNOWLEDGE

Example: **"OK."**

* If child (1) requires three holds or (2) refuses to comply after being in time-out for 20 minutes, use physical prompt to get child to comply to a portion of the command (e.g., physically take the child's hand and help him or her pick up one block).

Gets off before 5 seconds → Stays on for 5 seconds

HOLD CHAIR

Etc.

RETURN TO ORIGINAL COMMAND

Give similar second command and lavish child with labeled praise following minding.

DISCIPLINE PROGRAM HOMEWORK SHEET

Child's name _____

Parent's name _____

Did You Practice the Skills?

Enter Date	YES	NO	Time-outs	Length of holds	Prompts
MONDAY				1)_____ 2)_____ 3)_____	
TUESDAY				1)_____ 2)_____ 3)_____	
WEDNESDAY				1)_____ 2)_____ 3)_____	
THURSDAY				1)_____ 2)_____ 3)_____	
FRIDAY				1)_____ 2)_____ 3)_____	
SATURDAY				1)_____ 2)_____ 3)_____	
SUNDAY				1)_____ 2)_____ 3)_____	

Additional Comments or Problems:

THERAPY ATTITUDE INVENTORY

Child's Name _____ Parent's Name _____ Date _____

Directions: Please circle the response for each question which best expresses how you honestly feel.

1. Regarding techniques of disciplining, I feel I have learned
   1. nothing
   2. very little
   3. a few new techniques
   4. several useful techniques
   5. very many useful techniques

2. Regarding techniques for teaching my child new skills, I feel I have learned
   1. nothing
   2. very little
   3. a few new techniques
   4. several useful techniques
   5. very many useful techniques

3. Regarding the relationship between myself and my child, I feel we get along
   1. much worse than before
   2. somewhat worse than before
   3. the same as before
   4. somewhat better than before
   5. very much better than before

4. Regarding my confidence in my ability to discipline my child, I feel
   1. much less confident
   2. somewhat less confident
   3. the same
   4. somewhat more confident
   5. much more confident

5. The major behavior problems that my child presented at home before the program started are at this time
   1. considerably worse
   2. somewhat worse
   3. the same
   4. somewhat improved
   5. greatly improved

6. I feel that my child's compliance to my commands or requests is at this time
   1. considerably worse
   2. somewhat worse
   3. the same
   4. somewhat improved
   5. greatly improved

7. Regarding the progress my child has made in his/her general behavior, I am
   1. very dissatisfied
   2. somewhat dissatisfied
   3. neutral
   4. somewhat satisfied
   5. very satisfied

8. To what degree has the treatment program helped with other general personal or family problems not directly related to your child in the program?
   1. hindered much more than helped
   2. hindered slightly
   3. neither helped nor hindered
   4. helped somewhat
   5. helped very much

9. I feel the type of program that was used to help me improve the behavior of my child was
   1. very poor
   2. poor
   3. adequate
   4. good
   5. very good

10. My general feeling about the program I participated in, is
    1. I disliked it very much
    2. I disliked it somewhat
    3. I feel neutral
    4. I liked it somewhat
    5. I liked it very much

© 1974 Sheila Eyberg, Ph.D.

_____ Play therapy   **SKILL SUMMARY SHEET**   Child's Name _____

_____ Discipline   Parent's Name _____

	CRIT.	U.P.	L.P.	QUEST.	REFL.	DESC.	I.C./ N.O.	I.C./ COMP.	I.C./ NON.	D.C./ N.O.	D.C./ COMP.	D.C./ NON.	DEV. IGN.	DEV. RESP.
Baseline 1 Date:														
Baseline 2 Date:														
1st Coaching Date:														
2nd Coaching Date:														
3rd Coaching Date:														
4th Coaching Date:														
5th Coaching Date:														
6th Coaching Date:														
7th Coaching Date:														
8th Coaching Date:														

References

Abidin, R. (1990). *Parenting Stress Index manual* (3rd ed.). Charlottesville, VA: Pediatric Psychology Press.

Achenbach, T. M. (1991). *Integrative guide for the 1991 CBCL/4-18, YSR, and TRF profiles.* Burlington: University of Vermont, Department of Psychiatry.

Achenbach, T. M. (1992). *Manual for the Child Behavior Checklist/2-3 and 1992 profile.* Burlington: University of Vermont, Department of Psychiatry.

Barkley, R. A. (1987). *Defiant children: A clinician's manual for parent training.* New York: Guilford Press.

Barkley, R. A. (1990). *Attention deficit hyperactivity disorder: A handbook for diagnosis and treatment.* New York: Guilford Press.

Beck, A. T., Ward, C. H., Mendelson, M., Mock, J., & Erbaugh, J. (1961). An inventory for measuring depression. *Archives of General Psychiatry, 4,* 561–571.

Boggs, S. R. (1990). *Generalization of treatment to the home setting: Direct observation analysis.* Unpublished manuscript, University of Florida, Gainesville.

Butcher, J. N., Dahlstrom, W. G., Graham, J. R., Tellegen, A. M., & Kraemer, B. (1989). *MMPI-2: Manual for administration and scoring.* Minneapolis: University of Minnesota Press.

Campbell, S. B. (1990). *Behavior problems in preschool children.* New York: Guilford Press.

Campbell, S. B., & Ewing, L. J. (1990). Follow-up of hard to manage preschoolers: Adjustment at age 9 and predictors of continuing symptoms. *Journal of Child Psychology and Psychiatry, 31,* 871–889.

Clemens-Mowrer, L., McNeil, C. B., & Armstrong, J. (1992). Training foster parents to manage young behaviorally disturbed children. A poster presented at the 1992 joint conference of the Texas, Oklahoma, and Louisiana Psychological Associations, Dallas, Texas.

Conners, C. K. (1989). *Manual for Conners Rating Scales.* Toronto, Ontario: Multi-Health Systems.

Day, D. E., & Roberts, M. W. (1983). An analysis of the physical punishment component of a parent training program. *Journal of Abnormal Child Psychology, 11,* 141–152.

Dowdney, L., & Pickles, A. R. (1991). Expression of negative affect within disciplinary encounters: Is there dyadic reciprocity? *Developmental Psychology, 27,* 606–617.

Dunn, L. M., & Dunn, L. M. (1981). *Peabody Picture Vocabulary Test—Revised.* Circle Pines, MN: American Guidance Service.

Eisenstadt (Hembree-Kigin), T. (1990). *Parent–child interaction therapy with behavior problem children: An evaluation of overall treatment outcome and the relative effectiveness of two treatment phases.* Unpublished doctoral dissertation, The University of Florida, Gainesville.

Eisenstadt (Hembree-Kigin), T. H., Eyberg, S. M., McNeil, C. B., Newcomb, K., & Funderburk, B. (1993). Parent child interaction therapy with behavior problem children: Relative effectiveness of two stages and overall treatment outcome. *Journal of Clinical Child Psychology, 22,* 42–51.

Eyberg, S. M. (1974). *Eyberg Child Behavior Inventory.* (Available from Sheila Eyberg, Department of Clinical and Health Psychology, Box 100165 HSC, University of Florida, Gainesville, FL 32610.)

Eyberg, S. M. (1988). Parent–child interaction therapy: Integration of traditional and behavioral concerns. *Child and Family Behavior Therapy, 10,* 33–46.

Eyberg, S. M. (1992a). Parent and teacher behavior inventories for the assessment of conduct problem behaviors in children. In L. VandeCreek, S. Knapp, & T. L. Jackson (Eds.), *Innovations in clinical practice: A source book* (Vol. 11, pp. 261–270). Sarasota, FL: Professional Resource Exchange.

Eyberg, S. M. (1992b). Consumer satisfaction measures for assessing parent training programs. In L. VandeCreek, S. Knapp, & T. L. Jackson (Eds.), *Innovations in clinical practice: A source book* (Vol. 11, pp. 377–382). Sarasota, FL: Professional Resource Exchange.

Eyberg, S. M. (June, 1994). *Psychosocial models with young conduct disordered, aggressive children and their families.* Invited paper presented at the annual meeting of the NIH/NIMH New Clinical Drug Evaluation Unit. Marco Island, Florida.

Eyberg, S. M., Bessmer, J., Newcomb, K., Edwards, D., & Robinson, E. (1994). *Dyadic Parent– Child Interaction Coding System—II: A manual.* Unpublished manuscript. Gainesville, Florida.

Eyberg, S. M., & Boggs, S. R. (1989). Parent training for oppositional-defiant preschoolers. In C. E. Schaefer & J. M. Briesmeister (Eds.), *Handbook of parent training: Parents as co-therapists for children's behavior problems* (pp. 105–132). New York: Wiley.

Eyberg, S. M., & Matarazzo, R. G. (1980). Training parents as therapists: A comparison between individual parent–child interaction training and parent group didactic training. *Journal of Clinical Psychology, 36,* 492–499.

Eyberg, S. M., & Robinson, E. A. (1982). Parent–child interaction training: Effects on family functioning. *Journal of Clinical Child Psychology, 11,* 130–137.

Eyberg, S. M., & Robinson, E. A. (1983). Dyadic Parent–Child Interaction Coding System: A manual. *Psychological Documents, 13,* Ms. No. 2582. (Available from Social and Behavior Sciences Documents, Select Press, P. O. Box 9838, San Rafael, CA 94912.)

Forehand, R. L., & McMahon, R. J. (1981). *Helping the noncompliant child: A clinician's guide to parent training.* New York: Guilford Press.

Forehand, R. L., & Wierson, M. (1993). The role of developmental factors in planning behavioral interventions for children: Disruptive behavior as an example. *Behavior Therapy, 24,* 117–141.

Funderburk, B. W., & Eyberg, S. M. (1989). Psychometric characteristics of the Sutter–Eyberg Student Behavior Inventory: A school behavior rating scale for use with preschool children. *Behavioral Assessment, 11,* 297–313.

Funderburk, B. W., Eyberg, S. M., Newcomb, K., McNeil, C. B., & Eisenstadt (Hembree-Kigin), T. (1990). *Parent–child interaction therapy: Maintenance of generalization to the school setting.* Presented at the 98th annual meeting of the American Psychological Association, Boston.

Goyette, C. H., Conners, C. K., & Ulrich, R. F. (1978). Normative data on revised Conners parent and teacher rating scales. *Journal of Abnormal Child Psychology, 6,* 221–236.

Gresham, F. M., & Elliott, S. N. (1990). *Social Skills Rating System: Preschool level.* Circle Pines, MN: American Guidance Service, Inc.

Hanf, C. A. (1969). *A two-stage program for modifying maternal controlling during mother–child (M-C) interaction.* Paper presented at the meeting of the Western Psychological Association, Vancouver.

Harter, S., & Pike, R. (1984). The pictorial scale of perceived competence and social acceptance for young children. *Child Development, 55,* 1969–1982.

Kinzynski, L., Kochanska, G., Radke-Yarrow, M., & Girnius-Brown, O. (1987). A developmental interpretation of young children's noncompliance. *Developmental Psychology, 23,* 799–806.

Lipson, K., & Eisenstadt (Hembree-Kigin), T. (1993). Parent–child interaction therapy conducted in a Head Start workshop for at-risk African American preschoolers. Presented at the National Head Start Conference, Washington, D. C.

Loeber, R. (1990). Development and risk factors of juvenile antisocial behavior and delinquency. *Clinical Psychology Review, 10,* 1–41.

Loeber, R., & Schmaling, K. B. (1985). Empirical evidence for overt and covert patterns of antisocial conduct problems: A metaanalysis. *Journal of Abnormal Child Psychology, 13,* 337–352.

Luiselli, J. K., Suskin, L., & Slocumb, P. R. (1984). Application of immobilization time-out in management programming with developmentally disabled children. *Child and Family Behavior Therapy, 6,* 1–15.

Lyman, R., & Hembree-Kigin, T. (1994). *Mental health interventions for preschool children.* New York: Plenum Press.

McElreath, L. H., & Eisenstadt (Hembree-Kigin), T. H. (1994). Child directed interaction: Family play therapy for developmentally delayed preschoolers. In C. E. Schaefer & L. Carey (Eds.), *Family play therapy* (pp. 271–292). New Jersey: Aronson.

McGee, R., Partridge, F., Williams, S., & Silva, P. A. (1991). A twelve-year follow-up of preschool hyperactive children. *Journal of the American Academy of Child and Adolescent Psychiatry, 30,* 224–232.

McNeil, C. B., Clemens-Mowrer, L., Gurwitch, R. H., & Funderburk, B. W. (1994). Assessment of a new procedure to prevent timeout escape in preschoolers. *Child and Family Behavior Therapy, 16,* 27–35.

McNeil, C. B., Eyberg, S. M., Eisenstadt (Hembree-Kigin), T. H., Newcomb, K., & Funderburk, B. (1991). Parent–child interaction therapy with behavior problem children: Generalization of treatment effects to the school setting. *Journal of Clinical Child Psychology, 20,* 140–151.

Newcomb, K., Eyberg, S. M., Funderburk, B. W., Eisenstadt (Hembree-Kigin), T. H., & McNeil, C. B. (August, 1990). *Parent–child interaction therapy: Maintenance of treatment gains at 8 months and 1 and 1/2 years. Presented at the annual meeting of the American Psychological Association,* San Francisco.

Olley, J. G., Robbins, F. R., & Morelli-Robbins, M. (1993). Current practices in early intervention for children with autism. In E. Schopler, M. E. Van Bourgondien, & M. M. Bristol (Eds.), *Preschool issues in autism* (pp. 223–245). New York: Plenum Press.

Patterson, G. R. (1982). *Coercive family process.* Eugene, OR: Castalia.

Roberts, M. C. (1979). The effects on the model of being imitated: A review and critique of the literature. *JSAS Catalogue of Selected Documents in Psychology, 9,* 7–8.

Schopler, E., Reichler, R. J., & Renner, B. R. (1986). *The Childhood Autism Rating Scale (CARS).* Los Angeles: Western Psychological Services.

Schroeder, C. S., & Gordon, B. N. (1991). *Assessment and treatment of childhood problems.* New York: Guilford Press.

Shea, V. (1984). Explaining mental retardation and autism to parents. In E. Schopler & G. Mesibov (Eds.), *The effects of autism on the family* (pp. 265–288). New York: Plenum Press.

Shea, V. (1993). Interpreting results to parents of preschool children. In E. Schopler, M. E. Van Bourgondien, & M. M. Bristol (Eds.), *Preschool issues in autism* (pp. 185–198). New York: Plenum Press.

Sparrow, S. S., Balla, D. A., & Cicchetti, D. V. (1984). *Vineland Adaptive Behavior Scales (rev. ed.).* Circle Pines, MN: American Guidance Services.

Sutter, J., & Eyberg, S. (1984). *Sutter–Eyberg Student Behavior Inventory.* (Available from Sheila Eyberg, Department of Clinical and Health Psychology, Box J-165, HSC, University of Florida, Gainesville, FL 32610)

van Kleek, A., & Richardson, A. (1990). Assessment of speech and language development. In J. H. Johnson & J. Goldman (Eds.), *Developmental assessment in clinical child psychology: A handbook* (pp. 132–172). New York: Pergamon Press.

Webster-Stratton, C. (1982). Teaching mothers through videotape modeling to change their children's behavior. *Journal of Pediatric Psychology, 7,* 279–294.

Webster-Stratton, C. (1993). *The incredible years: A trouble-shooting guide for parents of children aged 3–8.* Toronto: Umbrella Press.

Wyka, G., & Gabriel, R. (1987). *Nonviolent crisis intervention instructor's manual.* Brookfield, WI: National Crisis Prevention Institute.

Index

Printed in the United States
36416LVS00002B/306

9 780306 449765